SOURCE
The Prentice Hall
ENGINEERING SOURCE

Introduction to the Internet
Second Edition

Scott D. James

Industrial & Manufacturing Systems Engineering Department
Kettering University

Prentice Hall
Upper Saddle River, NJ 07458

Library of Congress Cataloging-in-Publication Data

James, Scott D.,
    Introduction to the Internet
/ Scott D. James. — 2d Ed.
    p. cm.
    Includes index.
    ISBN 0-13-011037-X
    1. Engineering—Computer network resources. 2. Internet (Computer
network) 3. Computer science—Computer network resources.
    I. Title.
    TA158.7.J36   1998
    004.67'8'02462—dc21   98-36454
                                              CIP

Editor-in-chief: **MARCIA HORTON**
Acquisitions editor: **ERIC SVENDSEN**
Director of production and manufacturing: **DAVID W. RICCARDI**
Managing editor: **EILEEN CLARK**
Editorial/production supervision: **ROSE KERNAN**
Cover director: **JAYNE CONTE**
Creative director: **AMY ROSEN**
Manufacturing buyer: **PAT BROWN**
Editorial assistant: **GRIFFIN CABLE**

 ©1999, 1998 by Prentice-Hall, Inc.
Simon & Schuster / A Viacom Company
Upper Saddle River, New Jersey 07458

Printed in the United States of America

10 9 8 7 6 5 4 3 2 1

ISBN 0-13-011037-X

PRENTICE-HALL INTERNATIONAL (UK) LIMITED, *London*
PRENTICE-HALL OF AUSTRALIA PTY. LIMITED, *Sydney*
PRENTICE-HALL CANADA INC., *Toronto*
PRENTICE-HALL HISPANOAMERICANA, S.A., *Mexico*
PRENTICE-HALL OF INDIA PRIVATE LIMITED, *New Delhi*
PRENTICE-HALL OF JAPAN, INC., *Tokyo*
SIMON & SCHUSTER ASIA PTE. LTD., *Singapore*
EDITORA PRENTICE-HALL DO BRASIL, LTDA., *Rio de Janeiro*

About ESource

The Challenge

Professors who teach the Introductory/First-Year Engineering course popular at most engineering schools have a unique challenge—teaching a course defined by a changing curriculum. The first-year engineering course is different from any other engineering course in that there is no real cannon that defines the course content. It is not like Engineering Mechanics or Circuit Theory where a consistent set of topics define the course. Instead, the introductory engineering course is most often defined by the creativity of professors and students, and the specific needs of a college or university each semester. Faculty involved in this course typically put extra effort into it, and it shows in the uniqueness of each course at each school.

Choosing a textbook can be a challenge for unique courses. Most freshmen require some sort of reference material to help them through their first semesters as a college student. But because faculty put such a strong mark on their course, they often have a difficult time finding the right mix of materials for their course and often have to go without a text, or with one that does not really fit. Conventional textbooks are far too static for the typical specialization of the first-year course. How do you find the perfect text for your course that will support your students educational needs, but give you the flexibility to maximize the potential of your course?

ESource—The Prentice Hall Engineering Source
http://emissary.prenhall.com/esource

Prentice Hall created ESource—The Prentice-Hall Engineering Source—to give professors the power to harness the full potential of their text and their freshman/first year engineering course. In today's technologically advanced world, why settle for a book that isn't perfect for your course? Why not have a book that has the exact blend of topics that you want to cover with your students?

More then just a collection of books, ESource is a unique publishing system revolving around the ESource website—http://emissary.prenhall.com/esource/. ESource enables you to put your stamp on your book just as you do your course. It lets you:

Control   You choose exactly what chapters or sections are in your book and in what order they appear. Of course, you can choose the entire book if you'd like and stay with the authors original order.

Optimize   Get the most from your book and your course. ESource lets you produce the optimal text for your students needs.

Customize   You can add your own material anywhere in your text's presentation, and your final product will arrive at your bookstore as a professionally formatted text.

ESource Content

All the content in ESource was written by educators specifically for freshman/first-year students. Authors tried to strike a balanced level of presentation, one that was not either too formulaic and trivial, but not focusing heavily on advanced topics that most introductory students will not encounter until later classes. A developmental editor reviewed the books and made sure that every text was written at the appropriate level, and that the books featured a balanced presentation. Because many professors do not have extensive time to cover these topics in the classroom, authors prepared each text with the idea that many students would use it for self-instruction and independent study. Students should be able to use this content to learn the software tool or subject on their own.

While authors had the freedom to write texts in a style appropriate to their particular subject, all followed certain guidelines created to promote the consistency a text needs. Namely, every chapter opens with a clear set of objectives to lead students into the chapter. Each chapter also contains practice problems that tests a student's skill at performing the tasks they have just learned. Chapters close with extra practice questions and a list of key terms for reference. Authors tried to focus on motivating applications that demonstrate how engineers work in the real world, and included these applications throughout the text in various chapter openers, examples, and problem material. Specific Engineering and Science **Application Boxes** are also located throughout the texts, and focus on a specific application and demonstrating its solution.

Because students often have an adjustment from high school to college, each book contains several **Professional Success Boxes** specifically designed to provide advice on college study skills. Each author has worked to provide students with tips and techniques that help a student better understand the material, and avoid common pitfalls or problems first-year students often have. In addition, this series contains an entire book titled ***Engineering Success*** by Peter Schiavone of the University of Alberta intended to expose students quickly to what it takes to be an engineering student.

Creating Your Book

Using ESource is simple. You preview the content either on-line or through examination copies of the books you can request on-line, from your PH sales rep, or by calling(1-800-526-0485). Create an on-line outline of the content you want in the order you want using ESource's simple interface. Either type or cut and paste your own material and insert it into the text flow. You can preview the overall organization of the text you've created at anytime (please note, since this preview is immediate, it comes unformatted.), then press another button and receive an order number for your own custom book . If you are not ready to order, do nothing—ESource will save your work. You can come back at any time and change, re-arrange, or add more material to your creation. You are in control. Once you're finished and you have an ISBN, give it to your bookstore and your book will arrive on their shelves six weeks after the order. Your custom desk copies with their instructor supplements will arrive at your address at the same time.

To learn more about this new system for creating the perfect textbook, go to **http://emissary.prenhall.com/esource/**. You can either go through the on-line walkthrough of how to create a book, or experiment yourself.

Community

ESource has two other areas designed to promote the exchange of information among the introductory engineering community, the Faculty and the Student Centers. Created and maintained with the help of Dale Calkins, an Associate Professor at the University of Washington, these areas contain a wealth of useful information and tools. You can preview outlines created by other schools and can see how others organize their courses. Read a monthly article discussing important topics in the curriculum. You can post your own material and share it with others, as well as use what others have posted in your own documents. Communicate with our authors about their books and make suggestions for improvement. Comment about your course and ask for information from others professors. Create an on-line syllabus using our custom syllabus builder. Browse Prentice Hall's catalog and order titles from your sales rep. Tell us new features that we need to add to the site to make it more useful.

Supplements

Adopters of ESource receive an instructor's CD that includes solutions as well as professor and student code for all the books in the series. This CD also contains approximately **350 Powerpoint Transparencies** created by Jack Leifer—of University South Carolina—Aiken. Professors can either follow these transparencies as pre-prepared lectures or use them as the basis for their own custom presentations. In addition, look to the web site to find materials from other schools that you can download and use in your own course.

Titles in the ESource Series

Introduction to Unix
0-13-095135-8
David L. Schwartz

Introduction to Maple
0-13-095-133-1
David L. Schwartz

Introduction to Word
0-13-254764-3
David C. Kuncicky

Introduction to Excel
0-13-254749-X
David C. Kuncicky

Introduction to MathCAD
0-13-937493-0
Ronald W. Larsen

Introduction to AutoCAD, R. 14
0-13-011001-9
Mark Dix and Paul Riley

Introduction to the Internet, 2/e
0-13-011037-X
Scott D. James

Design Concepts for Engineers
0-13-081369-9
Mark N. Horenstein

Engineering Design—A Day in the Life of Four Engineers
0-13-660242–8
Mark N. Horenstein

Engineering Ethics
0-13-784224-4
Charles B. Fleddermann

Engineering Success
0-13-080859-8
Peter Schiavone

Mathematics Review
0-13-011501-0
Peter Schiavone

Introduction to ANSI C
0-13-011854-0
Dolores Etter

Introduction to C++
0-13-011855-9
Dolores Etter

Introduction to MATLAB
0-13-013149-0
Dolores Etter

Introduction to FORTRAN 90
0-13-013146-6
Larry Nyhoff & Sanford Leestma

About the Authors

No project could ever come to pass without a group of authors who have the vision and the courage to turn a stack of blank paper into a book. The authors in this series worked diligently to produce their books, provide the building blocks of the series.

Delores M. Etter is a Professor of Electrical and Computer Engineering at the University of Colorado. Dr. Etter was a faculty member at the University of New Mexico and also a Visiting Professor at Stanford University. Dr. Etter was responsible for the Freshman Engineering Program at the University of New Mexico and is active in the Integrated Teaching Laboratory at the University of Colorado. She was elected a Fellow of the Institute of Electrical and Electronic Engineers for her contributions to education and for her technical leadership in digital signal processing. IN addition to writing best-selling textbooks for engineering computing, Dr. Etter has also published research in the area of adaptive signal processing.

Sanford Leestma is a Professor of Mathematics and Computer Science at Calvin College, and received his Ph.D from New Mexico State University. He has been the long time co-author of successful textbooks on Fortran, Pascal, and data structures in Pascal. His current research interests are in the areas of algorithms and numerical compuitation.

Larry Nyhoff is a Professor of Mathematics and Computer Science at Calvin College. After doing bachelors work at Calvin, and Masters work at Michigan, he received a Ph.D. from Michigan State and also did graduate work in computer science at Western Michigan. Dr. Nyhoff has taught at Calvin for the past 34 years—mathematics at first and computer science for the past several years. He has co-authored several computer science textbooks since 1981 including titles on Fortran and C++, as well as a brand new title on Data Structures in C++.

Acknowledgments: We express our sincere appreciation to all who helped in the preparation of this module, especially our acquisitions editor Alan Apt, managing editor Laura Steele, development editor Sandra Chavez, and production editor Judy Winthrop. We also thank Larry Genalo for several examples and exercises and Erin Fulp for the Internet address application in Chapter 10. We appreciate the insightful review provided by Bart Childs. We thank our families—Shar, Jeff, Dawn, Rebecca, Megan, Sara, Greg, Julie, Joshua, Derek, Tom, Joan; Marge, Michelle, Sandy, Lori, Michael—for being patient and understanding. We thank God for allowing us to write this text.

Mark Dix began working with AutoCAD in 1985 as a programmer for CAD Support Associates, Inc. He helped design a system for creating estimates and bills of material directly from AutoCAD drawing databases for use in the automated conveyor industry. This system became the basis for systems still widely in use today. In 1986 he began collaborating with Paul Riley to create AutoCAD training materials, combining Riley's background in industrial design and training with Dix's background in writing, curriculum development, and programming. Dix and Riley have created tutorial and teaching methods for every AutoCAD release since Version 2.5. Mr. Dix has a Master of Arts in Teaching from Cornell University and a Masters of Education from the University of Massachusetts. He is currently the Director of Dearborn Academy High School in Arlington, Massachusetts.

Paul Riley is an author, instructor, and designer specializing in graphics and design for multimedia. He is a founding partner of CAD Support Associates, a contract service and professional training organization for computer-aided design. His 15 years of business experience and 20 years of teaching experience are supported by degrees in education and computer science. Paul has taught AutoCAD at the University of Massachusetts at Lowell and is presently teaching AutoCAD at Mt. Ida College in Newton, Massachusetts. He has developed a program, Computer-Aided Design for Professionals that is highly regarded by corporate clients and has been an ongoing success since 1982.

 **David I. Schwartz** is a Lecturer at SUNY-Buffalo who teaches freshman and first-year engineering, and has a Ph.D from SUNY-Buffalo in Civil Engineering. Schwartz originally became interested in Civil engineering out of an interest in building grand structures, but has also pursued other academic interests including artificial intelligence and applied mathematics. He became interested in Unix and Maple through their application to his research, and eventually jumped at the chance to teach these subjects to students. He tries to teach his students to become incremental learners and encourages frequent practice to master a subject, and gain the maturity and confidence to tackle other subjects independently. In his spare time, Schwartz is an avid musician and plays drums in a variety of bands.

Acknowledgments: I would like to thank the entire School of Engineering and Applied Science at the State University of New York at Buffalo for the opportunity to teach not only my students, but myself as well; all my EAS140 students, without whom this book would not be possible—thanks for slugging through my lab packets; Andrea Au, Eric Svendsen, and Elizabeth Wood at Prentice Hall for advising and encouraging me as well as wading through my blizzard of e-mail; Linda and Tony for starting the whole thing in the first place; Rogil Camama, Linda Chattin, Stuart Chen, Jeffrey Chottiner, Roger Christian, Anthony Dalessio, Eugene DeMaitre, Dawn Halvorsen, Thomas Hill, Michael Lamanna, Nate "X" Patwardhan, Durvejai Sheobaran, "Able" Alan Somlo, Ben Stein, Craig Sutton, Barbara Umiker, and Chester "JC" Zeshonski for making this book a reality; Ewa Arrasjid, "Corky" Brunskill, Bob Meyer, and Dave Yearke at "the Department Formerly Known as ECS" for all their friendship, advice, and respect; Jeff, Tony, Forrest, and Mike for the interviews; and, Michael Ryan and Warren Thomas for believing in me.

 **Ronald W. Larsen** is an Associate Professor in Chemical Engineering at Montana State University, and received his Ph.D from the Pennsylvania State University. Larsen was initially attracted to engineering because he felt it was a serving profession, and because engineers are often called on to eliminate dull and routine tasks. He also enjoys the fact that engineering rewards creativity and presents constant challenges. Larsen feels that teaching large sections of students is one of the most challenging tasks he has ever encountered because it enhances the importance of effective communication. He has drawn on a two year experince teaching courses in Mongolia through an interpreter to improve his skills in the classroom. Larsen sees software as one of the changes that has the potential to radically alter the way engineers work, and his book Introduction to Mathcad was written to help young engineers prepare to be productive in an ever-changing workplace.

Acknowledgments: To my students at Montana State University who have endured the rough drafts and typos, and who still allow me to experiment with their classes— my sincere thanks.

 **Peter Schiavone** is a professor and student advisor in the Department of Mechanical Engineering at the University of Alberta. He received his Ph.D. from the University of Strathclyde, U.K. in 1988. He has authored several books in the area of study skills and academic success as well as numerous papers in scientific research journals.

Before starting his career in academia, Dr. Schiavone worked in the private sector for Smith's Industries (Aerospace and Defence Systems Company) and Marconi Instruments in several different areas of engineering including aerospace, systems and software engineering. During that time he developed an interest in engineering research and the applications of mathematics and the physical sciences to solving real-world engineering problems.

His love for teaching brought him to the academic world. He founded the first Mathematics Resource Center at the University of Alberta: a unit designed specifically to teach high school students the necessary survival skills in mathematics and the physical sciences required for first-year engineering. This led to the Students' Union Gold Key award for outstanding contributions to the University and to the community at large.

Dr. Schiavone lectures regularly to freshman engineering students, high school teachers, and new professors on all aspects of engineering success, in particular, maximizing students' academic performance. He wrote the book *Engineering Success* in order to share with you the *secrets of success in engineering study*: the most effective, tried and tested methods used by the most successful engineering students.

Acknowledgments: I'd like to acknowledge the contributions of: Eric Svendsen, for his encouragement and support; Richard Felder for being such an inspiration; the many students who shared their experiences of first-year engineering—both good and bad; and finally, my wife Linda for her continued support and for giving me Conan.

Scott D. James is a staff lecturer at Kettering University (formerly GMI Engineering & Management Institute) in Flint, Michigan. He is currently pursuing a Ph.D. in Systems Engineering with an emphasis on software engineering and computer-integrated manufacturing. Scott decided on writing textbooks after he found a void in the books that were available. "I really wanted a book that showed how to do things in good detail but in a clear and concise way. Many of the books on the market are full of fluff and force you to dig out the really important facts." Scott decided on teaching as a profession after several years in the computer industry. "I thought that it was really important to know what it was like outside of academia. I wanted to provide students with classes that were up to date and provide the information that is really used and needed."

Acknowledgments: Scott would like to acknowledge his family for the time to work on the text and his students and peers at Kettering who offered helpful critique of the materials that eventually became the book.

David C. Kuncicky is a native Floridian. He earned his Baccalaureate in psychology, Master's in computer science, and Ph.D. in computer science from Florida State University. He is also the author of *Excel 97 for Engineers*. Dr. Kuncicky is the Director of Computing and Multimedia Services for the FAMU-FSU College of Engineering. He also serves as a faculty member in the Department of Electrical Engineering. He has taught computer science and computer engineering courses for the past 15 years. He has published research in the areas of intelligent hybrid systems and neural networks. He is actively involved in the education of computer and network system administrators and is a leader in the area of technology-based curriculum delivery.

Acknowledgments: Thanks to Steffie and Helen for putting up with my late nights and long weekends at the computer. Thanks also to the helpful and insightful technical reviews by the following people: Jerry Ralya, Kathy Kitto of Western Washington University, Avi Singhal of Arizona State University, and Thomas Hill of the State University of New York at Buffalo. I appreciate the patience of Eric Svendsen and Rose Kernan of Prentice Hall for gently guiding me through this project. Finally, thanks to Dean C.J. Chen for providing continued tutelage and support.

Mark Horenstein is an Associate Professor in the Electrical and Computer Engineering Department at Boston University. He received his Bachelors in Electrical Engineering in 1973 from Massachusetts Institute of Technology, his Masters in Electrical Engineering in 1975

from University of California at Berkeley, and his Ph.D. in Electrical Engineering in 1978 from Massachusetts Institute of Technology. Professor Horenstein's research interests are in applied electrostatics and electromagnetics as well as microelectronics, including sensors, instrumentation, and measurement. His research deals with the simulation, test, and measurement of electromagnetic fields. Some topics include electrostatics in manufacturing processes, electrostatic instrumentation, EOS/ESD control, and electromagnetic wave propagation.

Professor Horenstein designed and developed a class at Boston University, which he now teaches entitled Senior Design Project (ENG SC 466). In this course, the student gets real engineering design experience by working for a virtual company, created by Professor Horenstein, that does real projects for outside companies—almost like an apprenticeship. Once in "the company" (Xebec Technologies), the student is assigned to an engineering team of 3-4 persons. A series of potential customers are recruited, from which the team must accept an engineering project. The team must develop a working prototype deliverable engineering system that serves the need of the customer. More than one team may be assigned to the same project, in which case there is competition for the customer's business.

Acknowledgements: Several individuals contributed to the ideas and concepts presented in Design Principles for Engineers. The concept of the Peak Performance design competition, which forms a cornerstone of the book, originated with Professor James Bethune of Boston University. Professor Bethune has been instrumental in conceiving of and running Peak Performance each year and has been the inspiration behind many of the design concepts associated with it. He also provided helpful information on dimensions and tolerance. Several of the ideas presented in the book, particularly the topics on brainstorming and teamwork, were gleaned from a workshop on engineering design help bi-annually by Professor Charles Lovas of Southern Methodist University. The principles of estimation were derived in part from a freshman engineering problem posed by Professor Thomas Kincaid of Boston University.

I would like to thank my family, Roxanne, Rachel, and Arielle, for giving me the time and space to think about and write this book. I also appreciate Roxanne's inspiration and help in identifying examples of human/machine interfaces.

Dedicated to Roxanne, Rachel, and Arielle

Charles B. Fleddermann is a professor in the Department of Electrical and Computer Engineering at the University of New Mexico in Albuquerque, New Mexico. He is a third generation engineer—his grandfather was a civil engineer and father an aeronautical engineer—so "engineering was in my genetic makeup." The genesis of a book on engineering ethics was in the ABET requirement to incorporate ethics topics into the undergraduate engineering curriculum. "Our department decided to have a one-hour seminar course on engineering ethics, but there was no book suitable for such a course." Other texts were tried the first few times the course was offered, but none of them presented ethical theory, analysis, and problem solving in a readily accessible way. "I wanted to have a text which would be concise, yet would give the student the tools required to solve the ethical problems that they might encounter in their professional lives."

Reviewers

ESource benefited from a wealth of reviewers who on the series from its initial idea stage to its completion. Reviewers read manuscripts and contributed insightful comments that helped the authors write great books. We would like to thank everyone who helped us with this project.

Concept Document

Naeem Abdurrahman- University of Texas, Austin
Grant Baker- University of Alaska, Anchorage
Betty Barr- University of Houston
William Beckwith- Clemson University
Ramzi Bualuan- University of Notre Dame
Dale Calkins- University of Washington
Arthur Clausing- University of Illinois at Urbana-Champaign
John Glover- University of Houston
A.S. Hodel- Auburn University
Denise Jackson- University of Tennessee, Knoxville
Kathleen Kitto- Western Washington University
Terry Kohutek- Texas A&M University
Larry Richards- University of Virginia
Avi Singhal- Arizona State University
Joseph Wujek- University of California, Berkeley
Mandochehr Zoghi- University of Dayton

Books

Stephen Allan- Utah State University
Naeem Abdurrahman - University of Texas Austin
Anil Bajaj- Purdue University
Grant Baker - University of Alaska - Anchorage
Betty Barr - University of Houston

William Beckwith - Clemson University
Haym Benaroya- Rutgers University
Tom Bledsaw- ITT Technical Institute
Tom Bryson- University of Missouri, Rolla
Ramzi Bualuan - University of Notre Dame
Dan Budny- Purdue University
Dale Calkins - University of Washington
Arthur Clausing - University of Illinois
James Devine- University of South Florida
Patrick Fitzhorn - Colorado State University
Dale Elifrits- University of Missouri, Rolla
Frank Gerlitz - Washtenaw College
John Glover - University of Houston
John Graham - University of North Carolina-Charlotte
Malcom Heimer - Florida International University
A.S. Hodel - Auburn University
Vern Johnson- University of Arizona
Kathleen Kitto - Western Washington University
Robert Montgomery- Purdue University
Mark Nagurka- Marquette University
Ramarathnam Narasimhan- University of Miami
Larry Richards - University of Virginia
Marc H. Richman - Brown University
Avi Singhal-Arizona State University
Tim Sykes- Houston Community College
Thomas Hill- SUNY at Buffalo
Michael S. Wells - Tennessee Tech University
Joseph Wujek - University of California - Berkeley
Edward Young- University of South Carolina
Mandochehr Zoghi - University of Dayton

Contents

1

Introduction to the Internet

SCIENCE/ENGINEERING SPOTLIGHT: COMPUTER-INTEGRATED MANUFACTURING

Computers are tools that have been used to support the manufacturing process for a long time. For example, computers are used to order and maintain inventories, create job lots, and support the paper trail associated with these activities. Today, the manufacturing industry is taking a new approach to the employment of computers in the manufacturing process; in the future, computers will no longer merely support the manufacturing process, but instead be integrated into it.

For a good number of years engineers have been trying to create the "one-model manufacturing concept." This model is built upon the idea that any manufactured product is conceptualized, designed, prototyped, and put into production from one set of data stored on computer systems. These data comprise the actual geometry of the part (similar to a blueprint), manufacturing specifications (similar to a bill of materials), and machining instructions (similar to specifications for constructing the product). While the one-model concept is not completely funtional today, many companies have successfully embraced computer-integrated manufacturing and are taking steps that bring them

OBJECTIVES

After reading this chapter, you will be able to:

- Understand how the internet was created
- Learn basic Internet terms, including hostname, domain name, and TCP/IP
- Learn the basic rules for sending productive e-mail messages

close to achieving the goal of the one-model concept. With the widespread use of the Internet, it may not be very long before there are engineers working on the same electronic model of a product from several remote locations.

The Internet is an incredible resource that you, as a student, need to learn to use! How would you like to be able to do all—or at least most—of the research for a paper or project while sitting at a computer, simply grabbing the data from an electronic realm and massaging it right into the word-processing package with which you write? Do you have an old computer that is incapable of running any current software? Do you ever run into technical questions that no one you know seems to be able to answer, causing you to wish you had access to experts? If you answered yes to any of these questions, then the Internet is the place for which you have been looking.

Everyone talks about the Internet today. We are inundated with information about the Internet as we watch television, seeing commercials with www.this and www.that. Are you online? What's your e-mail address? Did you look at that company's Web site for information? These are common types of questions you may be asked today. The purpose of this text is to help you learn of the different services that are available on the Internet. In addition, you will learn some of the Internet jargon so that you may begin to understand and use some of the buzzwords that are flying around today.

This text makes only one assumption: that you have some type of access to the Internet. This book will neither discuss how to get connected nor every available Internet software package. These items are best left to your instructor, who can tell you of the specific resources that are made available to you by your school.

This chapter begins by examining the history of the Internet. A quick tour of the culture and ettiquette of the Internet is also provided, along with a discussion of the general advantages and disadvantages of using the Internet. The chapter concludes with a discussion of some of the more technical issues surrounding the Internet.

1.1 HISTORY

Soon after computers became commercially available in the late 1950s, there was an almost immediate need to initiate and promote electronic communication. In the late 1960s, the U.S. government realized the importance of enabling their research-and-development sites to electronically "talk" to one another. If the computers at various installations were connected, then files and data could be transferred much more quickly through those electronic links than by courier or mail services.

The government-funded Advanced Research Projects Agency (ARPA) created ARPANET in 1969 to allow military and government computer installations performing research to communicate over phone lines. ARPANET originally had four computers networked together, and this setup was destined to become the original model for the Internet.

Another key component of the Internet came from ARPA: TCP/IP. *TCP/IP* stands for Transmission Control Protocol/Internet Protocol and is a set of standards that describe how data are to be transferred between computers. TCP/IP is the "common tongue" that computers on the Internet must "speak". There are TCP/IP implementations for UNIX, MS-DOS, Windows, MacOs, and just about any other computer operating system you can think of.

Eventually, ARPANET, expanded to include sites outside of the government and the military; educational and corporate entities also realized the benefits of being able to pool computer resources and share information. This collection of computers all over the world—owned by individuals, companies, schools, governments, and military organizations—and the hardware necessary to link those same computers together form the Internet as we know it today.

A commonly asked question is, "Who runs the Internet?" No one person, group, or organization owns it. Its backbone is funded by the National Science Foundation in the U.S. In addition, there is an Internet Engineering Task Force (IETF) and Internet Advisory Board (IAB) that help to set standards for those who wish to connect to and use the Internet. The IAB makes its standards publicly available. These documents are known as RFC documents (Request for Comment).

Another organization, MERIT, which is based near the University of Michigan in Ann Arbor, Michigan, is empowered by the National Science Foundation to upgrade and maintain the physical network (wiring, modems, switches, and other related hardware items) of the Internet. It was MERIT that first suggested that the Internet should be allowed to carry commercial traffic.

The Internet is growing at an exponential rate: In the early 1980s, there were 213 hosts on the Internet; in 1986, there were around 2,300; today there are literally millions. June 1991 is another important period in the Internet's history, as it was the first time that the business use of the Internet exceeded its academic use.

The Internet has become so busy that the government started researching the idea of an Internet II in 1996. This new network would be used exclusively by government and educational facilities, while the original network would be used by businesses and home users.

1.2 INTERNET CULTURE

Initially, the Internet was designed to enable people to have access to computer resources that might not be available to them at their own private and work facilities and to allow the transfer of information between computers. Originally, the primary users of the Internet were researchers, scientists, and engineers.

Today, the Internet carries information—which could be in any format, from text to digitized video—on every conceivable topic. Everyone from your neighbor to the President of the United States has access to the Internet, which means it is possible for some people to have access to restricted information or other sources that they should not be able to obtain. There are computer crackers and other criminals using the Internet for their own illicit gains, just as elementary school children have found ways to watch satellite feeds from NASA.

You should cautiously choose the words that you use on the Internet—it is an electronic version of the real world in which you will encounter people from many cultures with many different perspectives. If you offend someone, you may get in the middle of a flame war (a term we will discuss later on). Just be aware that there are as many different types of people on the Internet as there are in the physical world; most users are friendly, but there are others who can be abusive.

1.3 GENERAL NETIQUETTE

There are certain conventions and jargon that have been developed for use on the Internet. If you read any of the many monthly magazines on the Internet, it may seem as though the 'Net has a life of its own. The following is a list of suggestions that will hopefully make your first experience with the Internet a bit easier:

- Use the *FAQs*. Many mailing lists and newsgroups put together FAQs (Frequently Asked Questions). Always get the FAQs and read them first, if they are available. Once you start using services like mailing lists and UseNet News, you will find references and instructions on how to get the FAQs.
- Avoid posting test messages. Do not waste people's time or Internet bandwidth with this kind of junk. You will find out if you can post when you try to post your first real message. If you absolutely must know if you can post, you should use one of the test newsgroups. See the section on UseNet News for details.
- Reply to questions. If you know the answer, share your knowledge. This is how the Internet has grown. If someone has personally e-mailed you with a question to which you do not know the answer, you should still send a reply stating your lack of knowledge, if only out of respect.
- Avoid *flame wars*. Flame wars occur on mailing lists and newsgroups when one person does not like what someone else has said. The second person then sends a nasty note back to the first person over the general mailing list, and the flame war begins. All that flame wars do is waste time and resources. If you really have a need to respond to a person that flames you, the least you can do is use private e-mail to send your reply, thus sparing the entire group or list from your personal disagreement.
- If you change electronic addresses, make sure that you unsubscribe your old address to mailing lists and update lists and resources such as InterNIC (see Section 1.5) with your new address.
- Abbreviations: Many messages on the Internet will contain strange-looking abbreviations. Here are some that you may run across, along with their respective meanings:

BRB (be right back)	<G> (grin)
CU (see you)	BTW (by the way)
FYI (for your information)	FOAF (friend of a friend)
IMO (in my opinion)	IMHO (in my humble opinion)
MOTAS (member of the appropriate sex)	L8R (later)
MOTOS (member of the opposite sex)	OB (as a prefix, obligatory)
MOTSS (member of the same sex)	PD (public domain)
OTOH (on the other hand)	ROTFL (rolling on the floor laughing)
SO (significant other)	WRT (with respect to)
RTFM (read the freaking manual)	

- Shouting: ANYTIME YOU TYPE IN ALL CAPS, IT IS ASSUMED THAT YOU ARE SHOUTING. If you want to make a °point°, type a special character, such as an asterisk (*), before and after the point that you want to make. Finally, "@#$%^" looks a lot better in print than real profanity; in other words, it is better netiquette to substitute symbols for obscene words or curses.
- Surfing and Lurking: Surfers are Internet users who cover a lot of Internet territory and typically are helpful to other 'Net users. Lurkers are people who use resources such as newsgroups, but do not respond to questions. There is nothing wrong with being either of the two extremes.

- *Smileys* or other emoticons often show up in text messages and are used to convey feelings. Here are a few such emotions and their meanings:

:-)	smiling	:-D	laughing
;-)	winking	:-(	frowning
:-}	grinning	:-]	smirking
:-I	indifferent	:-#	smiley with braces
:-{)	smiley with mustache	{:-)	smiley with a toupee
:-X	my lips are sealed	=:-)	punk rocker smiley
=|:-)	Abraham Lincoln	:-o	surprise
:-@	screaming or yelling	8-)	eyeglasses
:-/	perplexed	;-7	tongue sticking out

1.4 ADVANTAGES AND DISADVANTAGES OF THE INTERNET

As with most publicly available resources, there are both advantages and disadvantages to working with the Internet. The following two lists summarize the key points the two sides.

General Advantages to Using the Internet

- Information on the Internet can be accessed when it is most convenient for the user to do so. The Internet is never closed. Whether you work best at 3:30 a.m. or 3:30 p.m. the Internet is always available to you.
- The Internet is "blind" to race, religion, sex, and creed.
- The direct cost to most academic users is only their time. The resources on the Internet have been paid for by those organizations that are registered on the Internet and by groups such as the National Science Foundation.
- Since the primary form of communication on the Internet is writing, messages tend to be better organized and more productive than verbal communications.

General Disadvantages to Using the Internet

- Users must be cautious about the information they receive from the Internet—how creditable is it? Some people tend to believe that anything that comes from a computer must be right, however, it is important to remember that it is often other *people* who post this information, and these people may have made errors or may even be out to fool or con other users. In addition, computer viruses can be picked up from the Internet. See Chapter 9 for details on dealing with these issues.
- While the direct cost to academic users may be next to nothing, nonacademic users often have to pay for communications to the Internet through fees such as long-distance bills, membership fees to Internet service providers, and so forth.
- The Internet is fun, and therefore, it is addictive. People who would never ever think about wasting time at work or school can easily get involved in non-productive pursuits on the Internet that can add up to hours of time.
- Written communications sometimes may *not* be as clear as verbal communications. Some people are better speakers than they are writers. In addition, some people write messages, often of a derogatory nature, that they would be more reluctant to voice to a person when confronting him or her face to face.

- Mistakes can be amplified on the Internet. If you incorrectly state something on a mailing list, for example, several hundred (or even thousand) people may see it.
- Some people become information hoarders, quickly depleting computer resources such as hard drive space, printer toner, and printer paper and so forth as they record and save all of the information they pull off of the Internet. In general, if a piece of information was easy to get once, you can probably easily retrieve it again. If something that is important to you was difficult to get, write down how and where you got it. This method saves trees, your hard drive space, and your sanity from information hoarding and overload.

PROFESSIONAL SUCCESS: DEALING WITH TOUGH TOPICS

How do you approach learning, maintaining and digesting a difficult topic? It can be tough, especially if the topic is something that you learn early in your undergraduate studies, but have to apply later in your degree program, like calculus. How can you quickly refresh yourself with the material you learned without resorting to the 1,500-page calculus book you have not opened (or seen) in two years? For such a case, you should rely upon the pearls of wisdom from those who have gone before you.

I am a firm believer in creating little spiral-bound notebooks to capture the important information learned throughout one's college education. (Incidentally, I did not use this method throughout my undergraduate education. It was only when I went back to school to pursue my graduate degrees that I realized a need for this method, unfortunately.) Let us assume that you are taking your first calculus class to see how to apply this tip for success. Since you are taking Calculus I, in which you are learning how to differentiate, and you know that you will have to take Calculus II, Calculus III and Differential Equations, there is a good chance that you are going to need to go back and look up some of the information that you learned in Calculus I when you take the other classes. You should permanently capture the knowledge you gain in class, but not in the notebook you use everyday in your class. Why? Your class notes are usually quickly written, almost illegible at times, and are sometimes incorrect, because you or the professor missed a step.

Take the time after you have fully mastered a topic to write down what the topic is about in a separate little notebook. You should explain how the topic works, what it is used for, why it is used, and show several fully-worked example problems ranging from the simple and straightforward to the more complex situations you hope you will never see again. If you use this method as a regular part of your study schedule, you will be amazed later in your studies for three reasons: 1) You actually learned more material, because as you tried to concisely explain it in your notebook, you were re-exposed to it, 2) All of the knowledge you have is neatly organized for future reference, and 3) Preparing for exams becomes much more simple when you have a neat summary of basic information in front of you. Does this method really work? I have everything from Precalculus through Differential Equations in 256 pages in my "green book." When I had to review for an exam testing Calculus I through Calculus III knowledge, it was a breeze to look through the pages of my notebook instead of my calculus textbook of over 1,500 pages. I could not believe how many little things I had forgotten, and since I had prepared worked-out examples, it was easy to relearn the information contained within. I strongly recommend that you use this method for any topic that you will continue to build upon or need to apply to further studies in your degree. It really does work!

1.5 TECHNICAL ISSUES

If you are using your school's or company's computer resources, it is likely that the technicalities detailed in this section will be handled by a systems administrator in your Information Systems department. When reading an Internet or UNIX book, however, you will probably run across these terms at some point. Let us examine each of the terms and the various issues related to them.

Hosts   *Hosts* are computers on the Internet that provides a service (i.e., e-mail, file transfer, Web site, etc.). A host may provide a single service or multiple services.

Hostname and Domain Name   All computers that are registered on the Internet have a unique hostname and a domain name. The domain name identifies the entity to which the computer belongs. For example, the primary system at my university is *nova.kettering.edu*. The term *kettering.edu* is the domain name—it identifies that my domain is an educational entity (*edu*) belonging to Kettering, which is the school's name. The term *nova* is the host name, or computer name. The host name signifies a particular network or computer specific to the domain. Kettering actually has several computers that can connect to the Internet, and each one has its own hostname—for example, *nova.kettering.edu*, *defiant.kettering.edu*, and *corvette.kettering.edu*, among others. Some of the other extensions of domain names you will run across include:

.com (commercial or corporate entities)
.mil (military)
.gov (government)
.net (Internet access providers)
.org (nonprofit organizations)

The president of the United States is even on the 'Net at *president@whitehouse.gov*. Since the Internet originated in the U.S., there is generally no country extension added to the end of domain names of Internet sites in the U.S.; **.us**.may be added to the end of sites in the U.S., but if there is no country extension at the end of an address, then it automatically defaults to the United States. Internet sites in all other countries do require country extensions, however; any host name ending with **.fr** indicates the computer is in France, **.ca** indicates Canada, and so on.

IP Address   Most computers on the Internet have a hostname; all computers on the Internet must have an IP address. An IP address is a unique number that identifies a specific computer. These numbers are the means by which communications traffic gets routed to the appropriate computers. Without these numbers, there would be no electronic means to distinguish computers from each other. IP addresses for computers that are on the Internet are handed out by the Internet Network Information Center (InterNIC), with whom you must register to become a host on the Internet. (Your personal computer doesn't fall under this classification.) The number will appear as four groups of no more than three digits such as 192.138.137.2, which is *nova's* IP Address. Why have both hostnames and IP addresses? Hostnames are just convenient nicknames that we use so that we do not have to remember all of the IP addresses. When used electronically, all hostnames get converted into their unique and respective IP addresses for communication data-routing purposes.

Ports and Sockets   Every computer that provides a service on the Internet sends and receives signals over *ports*. For example, any standard e-mail connection will send and receive signals on port 25. It would not be advantageous for a computer to only allow one e-mail connection at a time; in fact, there may be times when multiple e-mail are sent or received simultaneously. How can this situation occur? The answer is through what is called a socket. Once a port detects that someone wishes to send an e-mail, the computer creates a socket for each particular user wishing to e-mail. This phenomenon is similar to the phone system in a company in that when you want to make a call, you pick up the phone. The phone system is responsible for locating an open line for you to use. The phone system listens for a phone to be picked up (port) and provides you with a line (socket).

TCP/IP   TCP/IP stands for Transmission Control Protocol/Internet Protocol. This term is a fancy name for the standard method by which all computers on the Internet communicate with one another. If you intend to be on the Internet, then your computer must speak TCP/IP. Essentially, TCP/IP breaks the data that is to be transmitted into little bundles called packets. TCP/IP sets the standards for what these packets should look like and how to transmit them between computers. In addition, TCP/IP sets standards for certain types of computer connections and applications such as telnet and FTP, which we will examine later.

UNIX   UNIX is a popular operating system for computers. It runs on everything from PCs to mainframes. Should you learn UNIX? Knowledge of UNIX does make using the Internet easier, as most of the original TCP/IP computers ran UNIX. Do you have to become a UNIX expert? You need to know no more about UNIX than you need to know about DOS if you are a Windows user. Most of the bigger sites on the Internet today still run UNIX, since TCP/IP is built into it. UNIX was designed to be an open operating system—a concept that embodies the idea of the Internet—so naturally, the two go hand in hand. Therefore, the more that you learn about UNIX, the better equipped you are to handle the Internet.

Client/Server   A server provides a resource (i.e., an e-mail server)—and a client hooks up to the server and uses that resource, for example, your PC—the client—uses your company's e-mail system—the server. While definitions of these terms may vary between textbooks and other instructional sources, the aforementioned definition is the easiest way to understand the client/server relationship.

SUMMARY

This chapter has provided a brief overview of the founding of the Internet and what electronic life is like on the Internet. While there are some disadvantages to using the Internet, its advantages more than compensate for its disadvantages. The chapter has concluded with a section that defined some of the common terms and technical issues that are often encountered when reading Internet material.

KEY TERMS

Address	Flame War	Netiquette
Computer	Hosts	Smileys
FAQs	Internet	TCP/IP

2

E-Mail and Finding Addresses

SCIENCE/ENGINEERING SPOTLIGHT: STEREO LITHOGRAPHY

How would you like to create an assembled product from some plastic goo? That is what rapid prototyping machines do. A specific type of rapid prototyping machine is the stereo lithography machine, in which plastic polymers are built up layer by layer and shaped with a laser. When the process is finished, a working plastic prototype of a product has been created. The most interesting feature of this method is that the prototype can have moving parts that do not have to be assembled. Some examples of items that have been created with stereo lithography machines include gear brains, bells with attached clappers, and exhaust manifolds. It is projected that by the year 2000, stereo lithography machines will be about the size of a laser printer and will be able to create parts with sizes of up to one cubic foot in volume. This advanced machine would allow designers to create the geometry of a part in a CAD/CAM package, send the design data to the stereo lithography machine, and, in a few hours, see a prototype of their design.

SECTIONS

- 2.1 E-Mail
- 2.2 How Do I Find a Person's E-mail Address?
- 2.3 Files and E-mail
- 2.4 Legal Issues and Etiquette Concerning E-mail
- 2.5 E-Mailing Outside of the Internet
- 2.6 Final Note on E-mail
- Summary
- Key Terms

OBJECTIVES

After reading this chapter, you should be able to:

- List several sources useful for finding another person's e-mail address
- Explain how text files differ from binary files
- Learn what types of documents should not be electronically transferred

This chapter looks at the process of sending electronic messages—called e-mail—to other people. It will discuss how to locate other people's e-mail addresses through a number of different sources that are available on the Internet. This chapter also examines how to send items other than text messages through e-mail. The chapter then concludes with some of the legal issues and etiquette that should be adhered to when e-mailing.

2.1 E-MAIL

E-mail (electronic mail) is one of the original uses of computer networking and communications. Put simply, e-mail allows you to send an electronic message to someone.

Whom can I e-mail?

- A single user
- A group of people
- A mailing list

What can I e-mail?

- A message
- A file (pictures, programs, etc.)

What are the advantages of e-mail?

- It is fast and efficient.
- It is cheaper than a stamp or long-distance call.
- You can create the message at your convenience.
- It is global in scope; the Internet is worldwide.
- Its electronic means save vast amounts of paper.

What do I need to be able to e-mail?

- The e-mail *address* of the person to whom you are going to send the message
- Your return e-mail address
- The message or file you want to e-mail
- Some form of e-mail program to perform the actual mailing. It may be a stand-alone program or part of another application, such as a Web browser.

2.1.1 A Sample Text-based E-mail Session

Many e-mail packages, such as PINE or ELM on UNIX systems or PEGASUS mail or EUDORA on PCs and Macintoshes provide a menu system that shows you the various available options. These packages also prompt you for information as it is needed. You should check out what e-mail packages are available for you to use and then choose one that you like. All e-mail packages basically require two pieces of information in order to operate: the electronic address of the person to whom you want to send e-mail and the message itself. Let us take a look at a sample session in which an e-mail message is sent.

First, I start up the e-mail package and tell it that I want to send a message (the bold type indicates what I have typed in):

```
Mailbox is '/var/spool/mail/sjames' with 0 messages [ELM 2.4 PL24]



    |=pipe, !=shell, ?=help, <n>=set current to n, /=search pattern
 a)lias, C)opy, c)hange folder, d)elete, e)dit, f)orward, g)roup reply,
 m)ail,
   n)ext, o)ptions, p)rint, q)uit, r)eply, s)ave, t)ag, u)ndelete, or e(x)it

Command: Mail
To: vjames@nova.kettering.edu
```

The e-mail package then puts me into an editor where I can type my message. Once I am finished typing it, I will save my message and then send it:

```
Hey V! I was wondering if you had a chance to look at the network
response problem yet.

Thanks,
Scott



And now: s
  e)dit message, h)eaders, c)opy, i)spell, !)shell, s)end, or f)orget
File /tmp/snd.19521 saved.
```

After sending the e-mail message, I can then follow the menu options to quit the e-mail program. Once the e-mail program has sent the e-mail to user *vjames*, she will receive notification that she has new mail. Let us assume that she reads the mail and sends a reply back to me. If I am on the system, I will receive a notice that says something like You have new mail. If I am not on the system, I will receive the notice the next time that I log in.

Once I receive a notice that I have new mail, I can enter the e-mail program to read it:

```
Mailbox is '/var/spool/mail/sjames' with 1 message [ELM 2.4 PL24]


 N 1  Aug 13 V James        (20)   System Response
   2  Aug 12 lblasdell@lite (43)   Graphics Problems...



    |=pipe, !=shell, ?=help, <n>=set current to n, /=search pattern
 a)lias, C)opy, c)hange folder, d)elete, e)dit, f)orward, g)roup reply,
 m)ail,
   n)ext, o)ptions, p)rint, q)uit, r)eply, s)ave, t)ag, u)ndelete, or e(x)it

Command:
```

I can now press the return key to view the contents of the message 1:

```
Message 1/1 From V James           Aug 13, 96 11:15:38 am -0400

Return-Path: vjames
```

```
Subject: System Response
To: sjames@nova.kettering.edu (Scott James)
Date: Tue, 13 Aug 1996 11:15:38 -0400 (EDT)

Scott,

I haven't looked at the problem yet. Hope to get to it today sometime.

V
```

```
Command ('i' to return to index):
```

At this point, I can return to the menu and quit the e-mail program by pressing the q key. Most e-mail packages that are available today have a very similar menu-based interface to make their use as easy as possible.

2.1.2 A Sample Graphical-Based E-mail Session

As previously stated, there are many graphical-based e-mail programs available. Microsoft provides a graphical program called Internet Mail as a built-in portion of Windows 95. Microsoft Office contains a program called Microsoft Outlook that sends and receives mail from the Internet. This section will examine a program called Eudora, which is a popular graphical e-mail program available for both Microsoft Windows and Macintosh operating systems. Just like most graphical e-mail programs, Eudora is very easy to use and has various convenient features built in. For example, Eudora displays a "mailbox" and plays a tune when the user receives new mail. The following is a sample screen from the beginning of a session in Eudora:

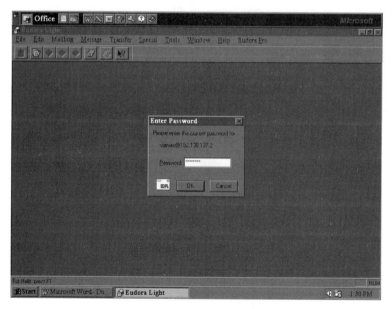

When a user wants to use Eudora, he or she user must log on to the system with a username and password. This entry procedure allows Eudora to confirm that only authorized users are reading their respective e-mail. After the user has successfully logged on, Eudora then allows the user to read or send e-mail. Working with Eudora is generally more intuitive than working with a text-based e-mail program.

Once I've logged in I select the "Mailbox" menu option, followed by the "Inbox" choice in order to read my e-mail. The following screen shows a list of the messages that I have in my "inbox":

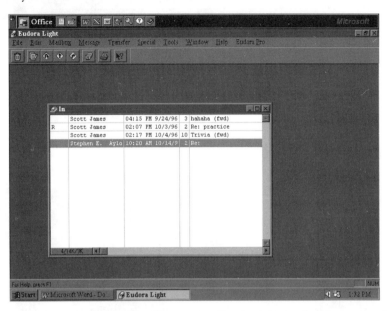

To read a message, I position the pointer of my mouse on the message and double click. Here is a screen containing the e-mail message that I received, highlighted in the previous screen:

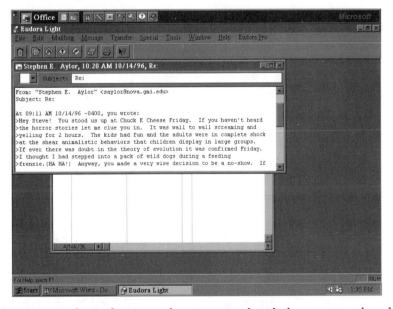

For most people, Eudora is much easier to work with than most-text based e-mail programs. Sending an e-mail message from Eudora is as simple as reading one: To do so I select the "Message" menu option followed by "New". The screen shown next then appears. From our discussion of text-based e-mail programs you should already be familiar with the information requested by Eudora in order to send e-mail, such as the

To:, From:, and Subject: lines. Once I have typed out my message, I click on the "Send" button to send the message.

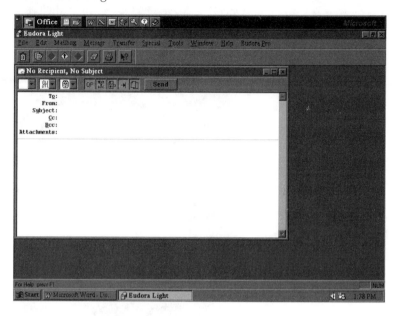

PRACTICE!

Try out your new knowledge of how to send e-mail by sending a message to a mail server that will e-mail a quotation from an almanac back to you. You should send the e-mail to the address *almanac@oes.orst.edu*. If your e-mail program requests a subject line, leave it blank. Some e-mail programs ask you if you want to continue with a blank subject line; if yours does, just answer yes. The body of the message should say send quote.

In a little while, you will receive an e-mail message back from the almanac server. You can read this e-mail using your e-mail program.

2.2 HOW DO I FIND A PERSON'S E-MAIL ADDRESS?

You will often need to locate another user's electronic address when sending e-mail. There are six different ways that you can try to find this information:

2.2.1 Finger

Finger is a fairly standard TCP/IP program that provides users with basic information about other users on a system. The typical syntax is *finger username@domain.name*. To use this type of locator, however, you either have to know the username of the address for which you are looking or at least the domain name of the computer that the person uses. An example of a finger command is *finger sjames@nova.kettering.edu*. This command will bring back information about me. If you do not know my username, but you do know the domain name of my address, you could type *finger @nova.kettering.edu*. Unfortunately, this command will return finger information for *everyone* currently logged in at *nova.kettering.edu*, including myself if I am on the system at the time.

You should be aware that not all systems allow users on remote systems to use the finger command. In fact some systems do not even allow their own users to use the finger command at all.

A Sample Finger Command

```
nova{sjames}1% finger @nova.kettering.edu
[nova.kettering.edu]
Login     Name          TTY   Idle   When       Where
khicks    Kim A. Hicks  p7    33     Fri 08:29  192.138.137.190
Jtandy    John Tandy    p8    3:39   Fri 07:39  tandy
hgholmes  Harry Gholmes pb           Fri 11:44  CURLY
sjames    Scott D. James pf          Fri 11:46  beopst
```

You can see that the last line of the feedback of the above sample command shows my username, my real name, the date and time at which I logged in, and the port name on which I am logged in, among other information. If you specify a username in the finger command, you can get detailed information on a particular user:

```
nova{sjames}3% finger sjames@nova.kettering.edu
Login name: sjames                In real life: Scott D. James
Directory: /faculty/sjames        Shell: /usr/local/bin/tcsh
On since Apr 30 11:46:48 on ttypf from beopst
Mail last read Fri Apr 30 11:46:51
Project: If you have to ask, I won't tell you...
Plan:
----------------------------------------------------------------
Scott D. James
Industrial & Manufacturing Systems Engineering Department
Kettering University   Internet: sjames@nova.kettering.edu
----------------------------------------------------------------
```

Sample Finger Sites to Try   The finger command can also be used to return more than just usernames. Some addresses offer lists and bulletins via the finger command. Here are a few examples of subjects and addresses that provide information about them when fingered:

Billboard Magazine charts: *buckmr@rpi.edu*

Nielson TV ratings: *normg@halcyon.halcyon.com*

Earthquakes: *quake@geophys.washington.edu*

Baseball scores: *jtchern@ocf.berkeley.edu*

NASA press releases: *nasanews@space.mit.edu*

Movie trivia: *cyndiw@magnus1.com*

Tropical storms: *forecast@typhoon.atmos.colostate.edu*

Northern lights: *aurora@xi.uleth.ca*

Coke machines: *@coke.elab.cs.cmu.edu*

M&Ms: *mnm@coke.elab.cs.cmu.edu*

Graphs: *bargraph@coke.elab.cs.cmu.edu*

Buy a Coke: *coke@cs.wisc.edu*

Almanac: *copi@oddjob.uchicago.edu*

Weather: *weather@cirrus.mit.edu*

PRACTICE!

Finger one or two of the addresses given above; for example, type *finger coke@cs.wisc.edu*.

2.2.2 Use InterNIC's White Pages Database

Though currently incomplete, the *InterNIC White Pages Database* may become the global address directory of the future. InterNIC welds several of the lookup utilities together under a common menu. To use the InterNIC White Pages, telnet to *ds.internic.net* and log in as *guest*; you will then receive information about how to search for a user. (See Chapter 4 for information on how to use telnet.) InterNIC's service is menu driven, so read the screens and follow the prompts.

If you want information about InterNIC, you can send e-mail to *info@internic.net*. If you want to add yourself to the InterNIC database, send a message to *admin@ds.internic.net* and ask to be added to the White Pages.

The following menu printout should give you an idea of what to expect when you connect to InterNIC (and after you survive the onslaught of questions about configuration, most of which can be answered by pressing the enter key):

```
InterNIC Directory and Database Services (DS) Telnet Application
                          Main Menu


        1) User Tutorial
        2) InterNIC Directory of Directories
        3) InterNIC Directory Services ("White Pages")
        4) Search the InterNIC DS Server File Space
        5) Browse the InterNIC DS Server File Space (GOPHER)
        6) Internet Public File Search (ARCHIE)
        7) Internet Documentation (RFC's, FYI's, etc.) Search
        8) End Application (or 'q', 'e', 'quit', or 'exit')


Enter option (1-8) or 'q' (to end session) and press <RETURN>:
```

2.2.3 WHOIS

WHOIS is the original InterNIC White Pages program and is one of the options available through InterNIC. To use WHOIS, you should enter as much of the person's name as you can when prompted to type in who you are looking for. If anything in the WHOIS database matches what you typed, that information will be returned to you. The easiest way to use WHOIS is to telnet to a WHOIS server. (A list of WHOIS servers can be obtained by anonymous FTP from *sipb.mit.edu*. The file */pub/whois/whois-servers.list* contains the information. See Chapter 4 for information on how to use FTP.) You can also telnet to *whois.internic.net* and log in as *whois*. Another WHOIS server that you can telnet to is *nic.ddn.mil*. (Start WHOIS by typing *whois*; there is no login or password required).

The second way to access WHOIS is to send an e-mail message with a blank subject line to one of the WHOIS servers, such as *mailserv@ds.internic.net*. The body of the message should be a single command of the following format: *whois -h hostname username*. The *-h hostname* portion is optional. By supplying a hostname, you can help WHOIS cut down on the amount of duplicate data it will return to you; for example, say you are looking for a user with the name of John Smith. Obviously, there will be many John Smiths, so including hostname will help to limit the search. If you only supply the username in the message, you may also want to put a period in front of the username, such as in the command *whois .sjames*. The period lets the WHOIS server know that you are requesting a person and not a host.

The third way to access WHOIS is to type the whois command directly at the prompt of your server. Many UNIX systems have a copy of this program, and using this method is more convenient than using Telnet or e-mail.

The final way to access WHOIS is to locate a gopher site that supports WHOIS searches. (See Chapter 5 for more information about gophers.)

If you would like to register in the WHOIS database, either download via FTP the file */netfile/user-template.txt* from *nic.ddn.mil* or get the file via e-mail by sending a message to *service@nic.ddn.mil*, with the file name *user-template.txt* in the subject line. After you have obtained the file, fill out the form contained within and return it by e-mail to *registrar@nic.ddn.mil*.

2.2.4 Netfind

Netfind does not rely on databases of information as InterNIC's WHOIS does. Netfind actually goes out onto the 'Net to access network gateways, asking if the gateway has information on the user who is being searched for.

Netfind requires two pieces of information: real name or login name of the person being searched for and a location for that person (a hostname, city, state, etc.). Netfind may or may not return any information, since some sites do not permit queries for this kind of information.

To use Netfind, telnet to *ds.internic.net* and log in as *guest*. After you log in, the system provides instructions on how to use Netfind.

Alternatively, many UNIX computers now run Netfind programs directly on their own interfaces. If you are on a UNIX computer, you might want to investigate this option, since it provides a convenient front end to a Netfind server.

Here is a list of some other U.S. Netfind sites that you can telnet to (login as *netfind*):

> *bruno.cs.colorado.edu*
> *ds.internic.net*
> *eis.calstate.edu*
> *hto-e.usc.edu*
> *mudhoney.micro.umn.edu*
> *netfind.oc.com*
> *redmont.cis.uab.edu*

2.2.5 Knowbot Information Service (KIS)

KIS does not maintain its own database; instead, it queries the other databases that are already available (finger, MCI Mail's directory, WHOIS, and so forth). By providing a single location for you to supply information on the individual you are trying to locate, KIS allows you to search multiple sources while supplying the information only once. All information returned is massaged into a single format so that all pieces are uniform in their presentation.

You can either telnet to a KIS server or e-mail a server to access the KIS service; for example, you can telnet to *nri.reston.va.us 185* to access a KIS server. The 185 is required, since this number specifies that port 185 on that computer is for the KIS service. Other KIS servers are available; a list is on the *nri.reston.va.us* computer. (Two other KIS servers in the U.S. are *info.cnri.reston.va.us* 185 and *regulus.cs.bucknell.edu 185*).

To e-mail the KIS server, send a message to *netaddress@nri.reston.va.us* or *mitwp@mit.edu*. The body of the message should contain one or more of the following keywords with the appropriate data attached:

- *Identifier,* the use of which specifies that KIS should use the information supplied after the keyword *identifier* for the search instead of a username. This keyword is often used when one specifies a user ID number instead of a name; for example, companies like Compuserve and MCI Mail use ID numbers instead of usernames, so one would need to use the *identifier* keyword when searching for someone at one of these companies.

- *Org* followed by either a full or partial domain name specifies the organization to which the person belongs.
- *Query* followed by a username specifies the username to search for.

An example of the body of an e-mail message sent to a KIS server is:

```
org kettering.edu
query sjames
```

2.2.6 UseNet User List

A server at MIT, where UseNet started, collects the name and address of anyone who contributes to UseNet News. Since many people read and contribute to UseNet, its data may be particularly useful for one who is trying to locate a user's address.

To query the list by e-mail, send a message to *mail-server@pit-manager.mit.edu*. The subject line should be blank; the body of the messaage should be *send usenet-address/username*. For example *send usenet-address/james* would return all UseNet users with the last name of James.

If you are not sure of the exact spelling of a person's name, you should include several send commands in the body of the message so that you can query a number of spelling at once. Doing so will help cut down on the amount of time you spend searching.

2.3 FILES AND E-MAIL

In the world of computers, there are two kinds of files: theirs (the computer's) and ours. Our files are nice and readable—for example, our e-mail messages. Their files are weird-looking combinations of characters that, as far as we're concerned, can not possibly make any sense. Examples of "their" files that are useful to us include graphics, sound files, and programs, but the actual files look like junk when we try to read them. This phenomenon is the concept of *text* (or *ASCII*) versus *binary files*.

It is extremely advantageous to be able to e-mail binary files. Say you wrote a huge spreadsheet in Excel on a PC in New York. Your Los Angeles office needs it *immediately* for use on their Macintosh. If you sent a disk containing the files by overnight mail it would take too long and someone would have to take the time to access the PC disk and convert the file for the Macintosh. You decide to put e-mail to the rescue. The only problem is that most e-mail programs will send only text messages, but the spreadsheet is stored in binary format. Text messages are what are known as 7-bit ASCII (the text is store as a series of characters from 0 to 127); binary files are 8 bit (stored as a series of characters from 0 to 255).

Your solution to this dilemma is to employ a program know as *uuencode*. Uuencode will take each 0 to 255 character in the binary file and convert it into two 0 to 127 characters. When this process is done, you can then send what appears to the e-mail program as a text file. When your colleagues at the office in Los Angeles receive the file, they will run a program called *uudecode* to convert the file from text mode back into binary mode.

- Let us look at how I would uuencode a spreadsheet called 1995sale.xls. I would execute the following command from my command prompt:

```
uuencode 1995sale.xls < 1995sale.xls > 1995sale.uue
```

This command uuencodes a file that will be called 1995sale.xls (the first filename) from a file called 1995sale.xls (the second filename) into a file called 1995sale.uue (the uuencoded file). Why are there two occurrences of 1995sale.xls? The allowance for two file-names (in this case, they are the same) permits computer systems that have filename limitations to work together. For example, consider the command *uuencode pcname.zip < alongunixname.zip > pcname.uue* in which the two filenames are different. Since MS-DOS files are limited to eight characters and an optional three character extension and UNIX files can have multiple extensions and filenames longer than eight characters, we would have a problem encoding files that originated in UNIX into files for MS-DOS if uuencode did not allow us to input two filenames.

The person decoding the file could then type:

```
uudecode 1995sale.uue
```

at his or her command prompt. The file 1995sale.xls will then appear in its original format.

- How do I know if a file has been uuencoded?

Typically, a uuencoded file looks like someone stepped on their keyboard while typing their e-mail message to you. For example, you may see something like the following:

```
This is the 1995 sales projection spreadsheet in uuencoded form.
-----------------------------------------------------------------
begin 644 1995sale.xls
M'XL1%329J-123(*#!!KA(SK(@KS(D(!@kd:!@ewe(!{!0]{ASDASD:)
ASDASKD!((QKQ*&KJ!@:L:!@"> @!{!(S(A*SI@*(SIAS(@(@I#
```

The first line reveals that the file has been uuencoded. 644 in the third line, below the dashes, is just a UNIX permission number that is not relevant to our purposes. You can see that the original filename appears on the "begin" line as well. This line indicates what uudecode should call the decoded file.

- A final note on file compression

If you have a large file, you should perform some kind of compression on it. If you have to send many files, you should put them into a single file archive and then compress it. The reason you must perform these operations is that an encoded file takes up double the amount of space used by the original file; for every character in the original file, two will appear in the encoded file. Therefore, compressing your files(s) saves a lot of valuable space. We will talk about common compression files in the section on FTP in Chapter 4.

Congratulations! You have just been named the secretary of your local science/engineering society. One of the regular tasks that you must perform is to make sure all members receive a copy of the minutes you take for each meeting.

Each member of the society has an e-mail address; so you have decided that you can simplify this task by e-mailing the minutes. In order to do so, you need to set up a group/distribution list in your pre-ferred e-mail program. In the example that follows, I use Microsoft Outlook, which is a part of the Microsoft Office 97 package. A compressed version of Microsoft Outlook, Microsoft Outlook Express is also included with Microsoft Internet Explorer 4. After starting Outlook, I must first add each person's e-mail address to my address book in Outlook by selecting "Address Book" from the "Tools" menu:

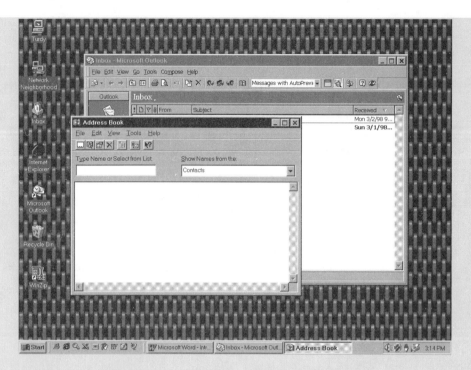

I access the "File" menu, select "New Entry", and then click on "Internet Mail Address" on time for each person I need to add to my list. Then, for each person, I fill in his or her real name and e-mail address:

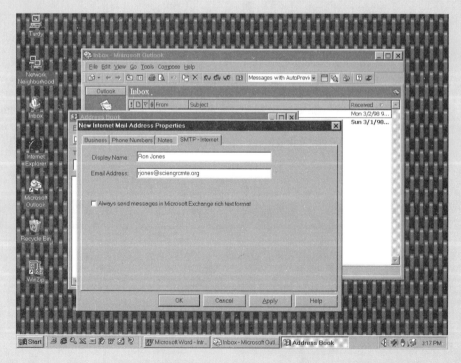

Once I have entered all of the e-mail addresses, I can create a distribution list by selecting "Distribution List" from the "New Entry" selection of the "File" menu and then add each member to the list:

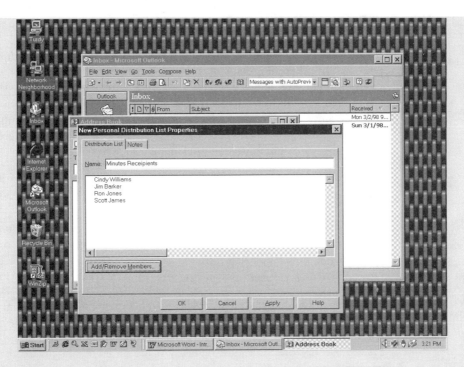

Whenever I want to e-mail a copy of the minutes to each member, all I need to do is send them to the Minutes Recipients list:

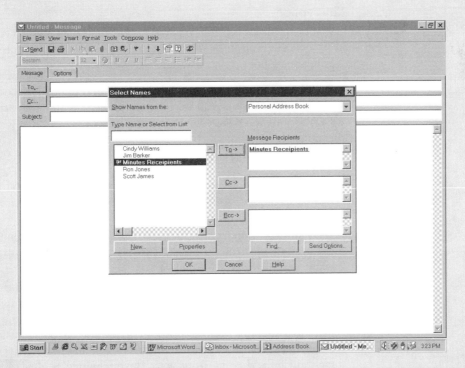

At this point, I can type the minutes of the meeting into the body of one single message and send it to each member at once using the distribution list.

2.4 LEGAL ISSUES AND ETIQUETTE CONCERNING E-MAIL

A note of caution: Anything you send electronically could end up in the wrong place or persons other than the recipient may somehow be able to view it. Various courts have ruled differently on issues of computer privacy. Some companies view e-mail and the use of their systems as company property. Even personal e-mail is seen as belonging to the company. Other companies feel that e-mail messages sent from employee addresses should be just as private and personal as actual mail. In either case, there are some definite no-no's: copyright infractions, mailing illegal material, and libel.

- Anything that is copyrighted should not be electronically transferred, since you are still making a copy of the original material if you send it, and that is illegal.

- Some types of material, even though they are not copyrighted, are illegal to send and receive, such as some forms of pornography.

- Libel, or slandering or defamation of a person's character, is as valid in electronic form as it is in any other.

The bottom line on e-mail legalities and etiquette is the following: If you wouldn't want anyone to see some piece of mail you have, just get rid of it! Be warned though, that deleting the mail from your account does not guarantee that it is completely gone. System backups of all files are regularly made on large systems. Also, there are some operating systems that do not physically delete files; they just mark the space taken up by the files as available, meaning that the deleted files could still possibly be retrieved.

2.4.1 Encryption

If you have a need for secure transmission of data, you may want to encrypt it before you send it. Typically, you first encrypt the file with an encryption program and then send it. There are a lot of programs available that do encryption:

- **ROT13** rotates all letters 13 locations; for example, A becomes M. This method is not a very advanced encryption scheme. You can duplicate the ROT13 program on any UNIX system that does not have it with the following command:

```
tr '[a-m] [n-z] [A-M] [N-Z]' '[n-z][a-m][N-Z][A-M]' < infile > outfile
```

- **Word substitution** requires the encoder to enter a keyword that locks the file into an encrypted format. The decoder must enter the same keyword before the file can be translated back to its original form.

- **DES standard encryption** packages use an algorithm to generate a code that is extremely difficult to break. This algorithm cannot be exported to most countries outside North America.

- **Public Key (PGP—Pretty Good Protection) Encryption** is a package in which you encode your message with one master key and individuals whom you trust are each given a unique key that will unlock the message. This method is superior to word substitution because the people who do the decoding do not know your keyword. This feature enables you to verify that the message did indeed come from you. This technique is also known as one-way encryption.

2.4.2 Etiquette

Just like any other form of communication, written or verbal, there are certain accepted principles that we use for electronic communication. E-mail is no exception! The following list is a set of good practices to follow when sending and receiving e-mail:

- Read your mail frequently.
- When replying, clearly identify yourself and the subject of the message.
- Make sure you write carefully, spelling words correctly and using proper English
- Know and respect your recipient; make sure you write only things that you would be willing to say when face to face with the person.
- Keep your messages to the point.
- Send e-mail only to those who need to receive it; in other words, do not send e-mail that is relevant to a select few people to an entire list of individuals.
- If you are replying to a message, reiterate the points to which you ar replying. If multiple people have replied to a message, include only the replies pertinent to the message to keep e-mail confusion to a minimum.
- Only mark urgent items as urgent. Some e-mail programs allow you to specify degrees of priority for each e-mail you send. If you mark everything as urgent, nobody is going to pay special attention to anything you send.
- Never assume that e-mail is private, as previously mentioned. Also, even if you send e-mail to the wrong address it will still usually end up somewhere—generally at *postmaster@domain.name* or *root@domain.name*.

2.5 E-MAILING OUTSIDE OF THE INTERNET

With all of the ways to get to the Internet, there must be ways to get outside of it as well. What happens if you want to correspond with an Internet-illiterate CompuServe user? This section addresses such issues. Let us first look at some of the more common computer services outside of the Internet, and then we will look at a list containing some of the less common ones.

America Online

- To send e-mail to an America Online user from the Internet, send it to an address in this format: *userID@aol.com.*
- To send e-mail from America Online to an Internet user send it to an address in this format: *username@domain.name*

CompuServe

- To send e-mail to CompuServe addresses from the Internet, send it to an address in the following format: *user.id@compuserve.com.* Make sure that you put a period in the user ID instead of a comma. Commas mean special things to e-mail programs, so we have to use a period instead.
- To send e-mail from CompuServe to an Internet user, you must include the word "internet" as part of the "Send To:" line—for example, you might send an e-mail to *internet: sjames@nova.kettering.edu.*

Genie

- To send e-mail to a Genie user from the Internet, send it to an address in the following format: *username@genie.geis.com.*
- To send from e-mail from Genie to an Internet user, send it to an address in this format: *username@domain.name@INET#.*

MCI Mail

- MCI Mail allows you to access users by their full name, username, or user number. Unfortunately, the user number is the only unique identifier. To send e-mail to an MCI Mail user from the Internet, send it to an address in the following format: *identifier@mcimail.com.*

  Examples of identifiers are:

  > *sjames@mcimail.com*
  > *scott_james@mcimail.com*
  > *139230@mcimail.com*

- For MCI Mail customers to send e-mail to the Internet, they must include the following information in their e-mail:

  > *To: person's real name*
  > *EMS: internet*
  > *MBX: username@domain.name*

Prodigy

- To send e-mail to a Prodigy user from the Internet, send it to an address in the following format: *username@prodigy.com.*
- To send e-mail from Prodigy to an Internet user, send it to an address in this format: *username@domain.name.*

2.5.1 Summary of Services and Required Formats

The following table provides instructions for communicating with some of the more popular non-Internet online services from an address on the Internet. This list is neither complete nor exhaustive. If you are interested in a more comprehensive list, access John Chew's Internetwork Mail Guide, which is downloadable via FTP from *ftp.msstate.edu* in the */pub/docs* directory.

SERVICE	SEND TO A SERVICE USER FROM THE INTERNET	SEND FROM THE SERVICE TO AN INTERNET USER
America Online	username@aol.com	username@domain.name
BITNET	username%site.bitnet@gateway Note: The gateway must be both an Internet and BITNET gateway	username@domain.name@gateway
CompuServe	nnnnn.nnn@compuserve.com	internet:username@domain.name
Delphi	username@delphi.com	in%"username@domain.name"
Genie	username@genie.geis.com	username@domain.name@INET#
MCI Mail	username@mcimail.com Note: users may have more than one nonunique name	Specify the recipient's name in the "To:" section, "internet" in the "EMS:" section and the full internet address (*username@domain.name*) in the "MBX:" section
Prodigy	username@prodigy.com	username@domain.name
UUNET	username%machine.domainname@UUNET.UU.NET	username@domain.name

2.6 FINAL NOTE ON E-MAIL

As you probably realize, sending text messages with e-mail is not a problem. We have to do some work up front to send binary files, though. There is a new standard that is being developed to solve this problem: *MIME* (Multipurpose Internet Mail Extension). In the near future, MIME will probably replace the Simple Mail Transport Protocol (SMTP), which is the current way that e-mail is exchanged.

MIME is not limited to messages containing only the characters 0 to 127. In fact, MIME specifically targets the following objects as items that should be sendable through e-mail: text messages, programs, audio files, encapsulated messages, multipart messages, videos, and image data.

Soon, e-mail users should be able to send just about any item through e-mail. The recipient of the message will then be able to "see" that item just as easily as we can see text messages today. The greatest advantage to MIME is that no form of translation, such as uudecoding, will be necessary.

SUMMARY

This chapter has provided an overview of the most basic, but possibly the most important, Internet services: e-mail. A discussion of how to locate the electronic addresses of other people on the Internet has also been provided. The chapter has concluded with an examination of legal issues and e-mail etiquette and instructions for sending files by e-mail. In addition, the chapter has showed how an Internet user can send e-mail messages to other computer services outside of the Internet.

KEY TERMS

Address	InterNic	UseNet User List
Binary Files	Knowbot Information Service (KIS)	Uudecode
E-mail	MIME	Uuencode
Encryption	Netfind	White Pages Database
Finger	Text (ASCII) Files	WHOIS

Problems

1. Send an e-mail message to your instructor to show that you know how to use your e-mail system.

2. Send an e-mail message to a friend at another school. Ask him or her to send you a message in return. Print out that reply.

3. Use the finger command and see if you can find out any information out about your instructor. Print out any returned information.

4. Print out a copy of this week's NASA Press Releases. You can retrieve it by fingering *nasanews@space.mit.edu*.

5. See if your instructor is in the WHOIS database. If he or she is, print out whatever information is displayed there.

6. Try uuencoding a binary file of your instructor's choice. E-mail the file to yourself and examine the message you receive. Save the message and then try to uudecode it.

3

Mailing Lists and UseNet News

SCIENCE/ENGINEERING SPOTLIGHT: OPTICAL COMPUTERS

Computers are getting faster with each new generation of microprocessors. Just how fast can they get? How about the speed of light? Believe it or not, computers that are currently available are constrained by how fast electrical pulses can run down the wires inside the computers. If the wires could be replaced by a material not subject to this constraint, computers could work more quickly. Optical computing is the answer to this dilemma. Light and fiber optics will soon replace wires. Even the switches that are integral parts of the computer may someday be replaced by light switches. So if you think that the increase in speed from the original IBM-PC's 8088 Intel processor to today's Pentium chip has been immense, watch for the greater speed increases that will result as optical computing becomes a reality.

SECTIONS

- 3.1 Mailing Lists
- 3.2 Using Majordomo Mailing Lists
- 3.3 UseNet News
- 3.4 Writing Postings: A Checklist
- 3.5 Alternative Ways of Receiving UseNet News
- Summary
- Key Terms

OBJECTIVES

After reading this chapter, you should be able to:

- Know how to subscribe to a mailing list
- Explain what UseNet is and who uses it
- Be able to receive UseNet news over email

This chapter examines methods by which Internet users may use mass text media to communicate with other Internet users. The Internet provides two ways for mass text media to occur: mailing lists and UseNet news. Mailing lists are collections of text items on one particular subject that are mailed out to all of the members on a list of subscribers. You can analogize this method to an Internet magazine. UseNet News, on the other hand, is the Internet's daily press. UseNet News has thousands of newsgroups and you can pick and choose which ones you want to read. Let's get started by looking at mailing lists.

3.1 MAILING LISTS

Mailing lists are another Internet service that you can use once you have e-mail access. The idea behind a mailing list is similar to that of the computer bulletin board systems that were popular in the 1980s. A mailing list is a location where people that have a similar interest can get together and discuss that interest. There are mailing lists on just about any topic that you can imagine. The method behind the operation of mailing lists is that you use your e-mail address to subscribe to mailing lists; periodically, you receive an electronic message back from that mailing list.

Some mailing lists act like magazines in that they gather together a number of messages and then send out one long message containing the respective texts of the several messages. Others will send out every message received as a separate text received from subscribers to each subscriber of the list. The general idea in either case is that people who are interested in a particular topic subscribe to a mailing list dedicated to that topic. These same subscribers typically e-mail messages, articles, etc. to the mailing list moderator, who, in return, has the mailing list server send out these messages to all of the subscribers.

The three primary functions that can be performed with a mailing list are:

- The list administrator can use it to deliver information to the list subscribers.
- Subscribers to the list can send out information to all the other subscribers.
- Subscribers can post files to the list or retrieve files that other subscribers have posted. (When posting files to the list, subscribers must remember to decode binary files before posting them.)

3.1.1 How Do I Find Which Mailing Lists Are Available?

You may download a list of available mailing lists via anonymous FTP from *rtfm.mit.edu* in the */pub/usenet-by-group/news.lists* directory, a site which is maintained by MIT. The list is in 14 separate parts, each with a name like *Publicly_Accessible_Mailing_Lists,_ Part_??_14*. You can also get a list back by e-mailing *listserv@vm1.nodak.edu* with the message *list global*. SRI has a mailing list that one can download via anonymous FTP from *ftp.nisc.sri.com* in */netinfo/interest-groups.Z*.

3.1.2 How Do I Subscribe to a Mailing List?

Once you know of a list to which you want to subscribe, you need to locate the list server that handles that particular list and notify the server via e-mail that you would like to subscribe. Instructions for doing so should be included in the source that told you about the mailing list. Typically, your e-mail message to the list server should contain a blank subject line, and the body of the message should contain the phrase *SUBSCRIBE listname yourrealname*.

For example, if I wanted to join the Thought For The Day mailing list on Texas A&M's LISTSERV, I would send the following e-mail:

```
To: listserv@tamvm1.tamu.edu
Subject:
Message:   SUBSCRIBE TFTD-L Scott James
```

If you are successful in subscribing to the list, you should receive a confirmation e-mail message. The basics of subscribing to list servers are that simple: All messages to the list server must be e-mailed, the subject line should always be blank, and commands may be entered in either case.

One other note of importance: When you receive messages from the list server, you will notice that its e-mail address is slightly different than the one you used when you subscribed to the list. For the example that I used above, I would receive a message back from *tftd-l@tamvm1.tamu.edu* instead of *listserv@tamvm1.tamu.edu*. What is the second address? It is the list address! If I send a message to the list address, everyone who has subscribed to the mailing list will receive a copy of the message. The first address is the list-server address that I use when I want to send commands (such as to subscribe) to the list server.

3.1.3 Other Mailing List Commands

There are several other commands that we work with when using list servers. All LISTSERV type of list server can provide you with help and let you know about the lists that they carry. In addition, most can tell you about lists that are carried by other LISTSERVs.

To get help from a LISTSERV, send an e-mail message to the server address with the sole word *help* in the body of the message. To find out which lists are carried by a LISTSERV, send an e-mail message to the server address with the sole word *list* in the body of the message. To request list information from the Texas A&M LISTSERV, I would send the following e-mail message:

```
To:  listserv@tamvm1.tamu.edu
Subject:
Message:  LIST
```

The returned message would contain only the lists maintained by the Texas A&M LISTSERV. To find out about all of the lists to which this LISTSERV is linked, I would send an e-mail message to the server address containing the words *list global* in the body of the message. I would then receive an e-mail back containing about 5,000 mailing lists that are available. If I want to limit the search a little bit, I could send an e-mail message to the server containing the words *list global* followed by a particular topic in the body of the message. For example, the command *list global business* would return any mailing lists dealing with business.

Some of the other commands that I could send to a LISTSERV type of list server include:

signoff listname	To unsubscribe to the list
register yourrealname	To register your real name on the server so you do not have to keep including it with every subscribe command

register off	To disallow your name from being reported to anyone who performs a review
review	To list the names of subscribers to a particular list
index	To show a list of files on the server. You can retrieve these files with the command *get listserv filename*.
info	To show a list of files on the server containing information about the server itself. You can retrieve these files by sending an e-mail message to the server address containing the words *info filename* or *get listserv filename*.

Note: You can include more than one command in a e-mail message. In other words, you may make more than one request from a server in a single e-mail message.

3.1.4 How Do I Post a Message to a List to Which I Am Subscribed?

Simply sending any message to the mailing list address (*not* the list server address) will get your message to the right location. The message will either automatically be forwarded to all subscribers to the list or go to a list administrator who gathers the messages, compiles multiple messages into a single message, and then periodically e-mails this compilation, which is formatted like a magazine to all subscribers to the list.

PROFESSIONAL SUCCESS: KEEPING IMPORTANT INFORMATION

It used to be relatively simple to find information on the Internet. Most of the people who supplied information on the Internet tended to maintain consistent e-mail addresses over long periods of time. Internet users felt that if they could find a particular set of information once, they could find it again. This situation no longer exits today, as people change their Internet Service Providers often.

My suggestion is that if you find information that is really important to you, you should download a copy of it to your local system so you will always have it. It is no longer satisfactory to jot down the system address of the location at which you found the information because that address may not exist the next time you try to access it.

When it comes to mailing lists or other systems by which information is automatically e-mailed to you, it is a good idea to keep a list of the commands that will unsubscribe you or cancel these mailings. It is a courtesy to update the mailing lists to which you subscribe whenever you change your e-mail address (unsubscribe with the old address and resubscribe with the new address).

3.2 USING MAJORDOMO MAILING LISTS

Majordomo lists are a different type of list server from the LISTSERV we examined in the previous section. This type of list is not as widespread as LISTSERV lists are. The concepts behind the use of the two types of list servers are almost identical though.

Here is a list of the most common commands for a Majordomo list:

subscribe listname yourrealname	To subscribe to a list
unsubscribe listname yourrealname	To unsubscribe to a list
help	To get help from a list
index	To show a list of files on the server

3.2.1 How Do I Find Majordomo Lists?

Sending an e-mail message to a Majordomo server containing the word *lists* in the body of the message will enable you to receive information on the lists carried by that server. An example of a Majordomo site at which you may start your search is *majordomo@vector.casti.com*. Another source of information on Majordomo list servers is the aforementioned files maintained by MIT.

3.2.2 Different Types of Lists

When you are obtaining information about lists, you may find that the lists are grouped into different categories. The most common categories and their meanings are:

Moderated: These lists are maintained by a moderator who reads and approves of all messages before they are posted to the list. Consequently, these lists stay focused and are sometimes more informative than unmoderated lists.

Unmoderated: All messages sent to the list address are posted to the list and, thus, are sent to all list subscribers. The main disadvantage to this type of list is that some of the postings may be unfocused, poorly written, or unrelated to the topic of discussion.

Digested: This type of list collects large numbers of messages and then periodically mails out a formatted presentation of these messages to the list's subscribers.

Undigested: The list server sends all messages out to subscribers as they are received. Subscribers to this kind of list run the risk of being bombarded with e-mail.

PRACTICE!

Find three mailing lists that you are interested in. Subscribe to one of them.

3.3 USENET NEWS

UseNet News is an organizer of online mailing lists. UseNet News was originally an experiment that took place at the University of North Carolina in 1979. Today there are literally millions of people who use UseNet daily, and for many, their perceptions of the Internet are formed solely from this experience. UseNet is really nothing more than a mechanism that allows groups to be formed and facilitates discussions within them. An advantage of UseNet is that the user can pick which groups he or she wants to view and will see news messages as they are posted.

There are now more than 10,000 *newsgroups* on topics ranging from motorcycle repair to the newest Microsoft products. If you are interested in a particular topic, you are likely to find a newsgroup to your liking. Since computer resources are limited, archives of postings on these groups are usually kept for only two weeks or so. Thus, if you see an article in which you are interested, you should read or download it while you can.

UseNet is an extremely valuable resource. Since each group is dedicated to a specific topic, you can ask technical questions on the group and receive responses from other individuals who are active and knowledgeable in that particular area.

UseNet does not physically exist anywhere. Its existence is similar to the concept behind LISTSERV; i.e., there are news servers. Essentially, you use a news-reader software that lets you read messages, post messages, and access the different groups. It is very much like e-mail in that regard. UseNet does not automatically send postings to your mailbox, however; it is your responsibility to read the news and download what you want to keep. UseNet does support the uuencoding and uudecoding of binary files, so those types of files can be posted to a particular newsgroup.

Newsgroups typically have "threads" running through them. A thread begins when someone asks a question and then receives replies to that question. When other users start replying to the first reply, a thread is born.

Sometimes, threads and flame wars on newsgroups get out of hand. It is important to know the capabilities of your *news reader* in such a situation. For example, many news readers allow "killfiles" to be created. Killfiles are used to screen out threads or words or phrases that you do not want to see. It is useful to know whether or not your news reader allows killfiles when there are sets of postings that are irrelevant to or too time consuming for your purposes.

3.3.1 A Few Newsgroups

Here is a very small sampling of some the newsgroups that are available:

misc.forsale	comp.unix.questions	comp.lang.c
rec.arts.movies	alt.folklore.urban	misc.education
misc.invest	alt.business.import-export	

3.3.2 What Is In a Group Name?

Most groups have some prefix attached to them, as you can tell from the above examples. Here is a list of the most common prefixes and what they mean:

- alt: usually somewhat of an "underground" newsgroup, such as alt.tasteless; however, there are excellent alt groups, such as alt.3d, which has regular discussions on radiosity and ray tracing
- bionet: biology
- bit: topics from Bitnet
- biz: business, marketing, and advertisements
- clari: Clarinet is real news provided by a private company. Access to this news must be paid for, usually by the news server that wishes to carry these groups. In fact, in most cases, if you see any clari groups, someone has most likely paid for these groups to be carried on the server for you, so feel free to use them without worring about being charged.
- comp: computers
- gnu: Free Software Foundation and its GNU project
- ieee: Institute of Electrical and Electronic Engineering
- k12: kindergarten through high school
- misc: newsgroups that do not fall into one of the other categories
- news: general news and topical items about UseNet itself
- rec: recreation, hobbies, and the arts

- sci: science
- soc: social issues
- talk: debate oriented

Some newsgroups are jokes and may only appear for a day or two. An odd group name like *alt.swedish.chef.bork.bork.bork* probably is a joke.

There are also moderated newsgroups, which are just like moderated mailing lists. The group moderator sorts out the messages before they are posted on the group. This system tends to keep discussion on track, keep conversation tasteful, and prevent flame wars.

3.3.3 How Do I Get Started on UseNet?

Once you have a news reader and point it toward a news server, it will probably have access to literally thousands of newsgroups, many of which you will not be interested in. Don't worry—you can unsubscribe to the ones that you do not want. There are several groups that you might want to examine for help in getting started with using UseNet News: *news.announce.newusers, news.answers, news.groups, news.newusers.questions,* and *news.software.*

news.announce.newusers regularly posts five articles that are of interest to new users:

- Answers to frequently asked questions about UseNet
- A primer on how to work with the UseNet community
- Rules for posting to UseNet
- Hints for writing style for UseNet
- Emily Postnews answers your questions on netiquette

news.answers serves two purposes for us: First, we can post questions about UseNet, and second, we can find almost all of the other newsgroups' FAQs.

3.3.4 What Are the Common Tasks I Can Perform on UseNet?

The answer to this question is going to depend more on the news reader that you use than on anything else. You should be able to do the following tasks with most readers: read articles, post articles, uudecode articles, and subscribe or unsubscribe to groups. Let us take a quick look at some of these features.

When you choose to post an article, make sure your posting is well written, clear, concise, spell checked and that it does not ramble. (These rules sound like the same ones we set up for e-mail messages). Adhering to these guidelines is important so that users who have to pay for their news connections do not pull down long and pointless postings.

Make sure that the posting is well laid out by keeping line lengths between 60 and 65 characters long. Also, if the message is long, you should state that fact by typing "(long)" in the subject area of the article.

Make sure that you do not post graphics or other binary files to a newsgroup that is text based. There are groups that exist purely for binary files. (Remember that binary files must be uuencoded.) Also do not post test messages to groups. If you absolutely, positively must do so, post to either *misc.test* or *alt.test*, where you will not annoy anyone. You will receive an automatic e-mail reply if your test message was successful.

Finally, end your messages with a signature, if you want. Many news readers and e-mail programs will allow you to create a *signature file* that is automatically appended to anything that you post or send. A signature is a very convenient way to let others know your name and e-mail address. You should try to limit this signature to three or four lines long. My signature is:

```
-----------------------------------------------------------
Scott D. James
e-mail: sjames@nova.kettering.edu
Industrial & Manufacturing Systems Engineering
Kettering University              phone:   (810) 762-9859
Flint, Michigan                   fax:     (810) 762-9924
```

Remember to keep your signature short; many groups will not accept postings with long signatures. A lot of users' signatures end with a humorous (but not obnoxious) saying or quote.

Watch out for anonymous postings. If your service provides the capability to make anonymous postings, you should seldom (if ever) use it. Why? If you want to say something, you should be brave enough to attach your name to it. Secondly, the fact that a posting is anonymous just means the message does not have your name or e-mail address in it; there is still an electronic log of an incoming message from your site that could be traced should it become necessary to do so.

Cross-posting is another issue with which you should be careful. Cross-posting is sending a single article to multiple groups. Unfortunately, some people send articles to the wrong groups as well as those that should receive them. If someone so purposely, his or her action is called "spamming." One example of a spam that circulates fairly regularly on most of the newgroups is the e-mail about a "get-rich-quick pyramid scheme."

Replying to a post is fairly easy, as the news reader will fill in all of the header information from the original article's header. Most readers will also include the original message in a reply. You should prune this part down to the important parts only and then write in your reply.

APPLICATION:
USING USENET NEWS AS AN INFORMATION SOURCE

Since UseNet News contains a wealth of information, you can often use it to find sources for somewhat obscure topics. In this example, I need to find out if anyone knows the file format that AutoDesk uses for its 3D Studio product. I need this information because I have to write a file translator that will read 3D Studio files for one of my clients. I will check UseNet News to see if anyone has already posted this information.

First, I need to start up a news reader. I use the *nn* reader that runs on my UNIX system. Most web browsers also provide support for reading the news, and there are several graphical-based news readers.

```
defiant{sjames}7% nn
Connecting to NNTP server zip.eecs.umich.edu ...
Connecting to NNTP server zip.eecs.umich.edu ... ok (posting is allowed)
Release 6.5b3.0 #6 (NOV),  Kim F. Storm, 1991
```

Once *nn* is running, the newsgroup that I most commonly read is shown first. In this example, it is *alt.3d*, which is a newsgroup that deals with three-dimensional software systems. You can also see that there just over 1,000 articles to view in this newsgroup.

```
Reading alt.3d: 1025 articles
a   F X DeJesus        29   >>Chinalake WWW Site
b   F X DeJesus        13   >>MESHPAINT WHERE!!!!????
c   Dean Fogarty       13   Animation Master : any users ?
d   Juergen Fechter    15   >3DMAX View Star glasses
e   Neal G Thomas      10   >3d Model of Enterprise 1701d
f   Jack Campbell       8   New Low prices Print Posters 24x36 $12
g   SGiff68285          5   >Carreer as a special effects artist
h   James Fences        9   >3DS file formats
i   Dino Pannozzo       9   3D-Studio: does box-mapping also work for flat
j   Empty              14   >>>Product Info Needed
k   Jack Campbell      13   Poster from your pictures 24x36$12
l   Eric Klien         28   Oceania
m   giorgio natale      3   View Master
n   giorgio natale      3
o   giorgio natale      3   >3DS to Wavefront
p   Ben F M School      1   TEST
q   MT                  1   -
r   MT                  1   -


12:05 -- SELECT -- help:? -----Top 16%-----
```

I have been shown the first page of a listing of the 1,025 articles. I can then select whichever articles I want to read. Next I choose to read an article immediately and return to the group to choose more or to finish selecting all of the articles that I want to see out of the 1,025 and view them all at once.

You should also notice that the last line of the screen shows that I can get help by pressing the ? character. The page of article subjects that I am viewing is the first 16% of the 1,025 articles. I can move from page to page by pressing the space key. I select articles by typing the letter that precedes the article's author.

The subject line of article *h* looks promising, so I select article *h* and immediately read it:

```
Sat, 8 Apr 95 17:51
>3DS file formats


>Does anyone have the file format that 3D studio uses?
You might want to see if AutoDesk has an ftp site.
Also, O'Reilly & Associates has a book called the Encyclopedia of
Computer Graphics Format or some such thing that probably has the
format.


Regards,
Jim
```

The article posted by Jim Fences is a reply to someone who apparently wanted to know about the format that AutoDesk's 3D Studio uses to save its files, which is the same information for which I am looking. From the article, I am given the name of a book that may contain the file format. If the book does not contain the appropriate information, I could try e-mailing Jim Fences personally, since he answered the original question and may have some expertise in that area.

3.4 WRITING POSTINGS: A CHECKLIST

Here are a few suggestions that you might want to follow when posting messages to a newsgroup on UseNet News:

- Make sure you are posting to the proper newsgroup(s).
- Make sure your posting is concise, spell checked, and uses proper English.
- People are not going to remember everything they have read. Paraphrase the text to which you are replying.
- If you are asking for help with a software program, make sure you mention the type of computer system on which it is running and which version of the program you have.
- Do not post a message that says, "when you reply, send a personal e-mail; I don't read this group." If you have a question, chances are that someone else has the same question and would benefit from the answer. In addition, if you do not read the group, what are you doing posting on it?

PRACTICE!

Find out if you have access to a news reader program. If you do use the news reader to browse through the available newsgroups. Read some articles from a newsgroup that interests you.

3.5 ALTERNATIVE WAYS OF RECEIVING USENET NEWS

If you do not have access to a news reader, there are a couple of other ways that you can get UseNet News. This section will examine these ways.

3.5.1 E-Mail

If you want, you can receive selected news through e-mail. This method can be advantageous if you do not have the time to run through a news reader. Stanford University has a news-filtering service in which you can send an e-mail message requesting what you are looking for. The service will then scan the news and mail any related postings to you.

The address for this service is *netnews@db.stanford.edu*, and the message body of a request sent to this address takes the following form:

subscribe <keywords>	the subject you're looking for—i.e., subscribe 3D graphics
period <frequency>	how often you want to receive mail, in days—i.e., period 3
threshold <frequency>	how well it has to relate to keywords (0–100%) this command is optional
expire <frequency>	when you want the service to stop, in days—this command is optional

So, if I want to have all of the articles that exactly match the criteria "computer graphics" bundled up and sent to me every four days and I want this service to stop in 12 days, I should send the following e-mail message:

```
defiant{sjames}8%mail netnews@db.stanford.edu
subscribe computer graphics
```

```
threshold 100
period 4
expire 12
```

Note that you can also check the news.answers newsgroup for more information on this service.

3.5.2 Gopher

Some gopher sites carry partial UseNet News, such as *info.latech.edu, pinchy.micro.umn.edu* and *src.doc.ic.ac.uk*. The advantage to using gopher is that there are several public gopher sites that are available, while there are few public news server sites. The disadvantages to using gopher to read the news include the fact that most gopher sites do not allow posting capabilities and most have limited threading capabilities. Gophers are discussed in Chapter 5.

3.5.3 Web Browsers

Most Web browsers allow you to specify an NNTP_Server (news server) in their configuration. Once you do so, you can usually specify the newsgroup name in the URL space, following the format *news:newsgroup*. See Chapter 6 for more information on Web browsers and URLs.

SUMMARY

This chapter has looked at the original mass media communications available on the Internet: mailing lists and UseNet News. The chapter has provided coverage of how to subscribe, unsubscribe, and post to both LISTSERV- and Majordomo-type mailing lists. The chapter has also examined UseNet newsgroups and the common tasks performed with them. The chapter has concluded with an examination of alternative ways of getting UseNet News without a news reader.

KEY TERMS

Digested	Newsgroup	Unmoderated
LISTSERV	News Reader	Unsubscribing
Mailing Lists	Signature File	UseNet News
Majordomo	Subscribing	
Moderated	Undigested	

Problems

1. Try subscribing to a mailing list. You can either get a copy of the news.lists directory or try one from the following list:
   CAD Mailing List:
   List Address: *cadam-l@suvm.syr.edu*
   Subscription Address: *listserv@suvm.syr.edu*
   History Mailing List:
   List Address: *hist-l@rutvm1.rutgers.edu*
   Subscription Address: *listserv@rutvm1.rutgers.edu*
   Net Happenings List:
   List Address: *net-happenings@is.internic.net*
   Subscription Address: *listserv@is.internic.net*

2. Print out your subscription notification e-mail message. You can then unsubscribe from the list if you want.

3. Use your news reader to join a newsgroup. Print out any article from that newsgroup that you thought was interesting.

4

Telnet, FTP, and Locating Files

SCIENCE/ENGINEERING SPOTLIGHT: NANOTECHNOLOGY

Imagine someone having a heart attack for which the hospital personnel are able to determine the extent of the damage and repair it without performing a catheterization. Even thought it sounds like sci-fi, the prospect of such medical advantages is on the horizon with nanotechnology. Nanotechnology is the creation of extremely minute machines that can have motors, tools, and computers built into them. In the aforementioned scenario, the hospital personnel could inject a nanomachine, equipped with a microscopic video camera and perhaps a laser, into the patient's blood stream. The video camera could send back images of the heart damage, while the laser could remove the plaque that caused the heart attack from the artery walls. After the nanomachine completes its work, it could be either removed from a predetermined location in the patient's body or left in the bloodstream to be naturally purged by the body.

OBJECTIVES

After reading this chapter, you should be able to:

- Know how to use Telnet
- Download and a upload a document at an FTP site
- List the different types of file extensions and know what they signify

This chapter begins by examining how to access computers on the Internet via the telnet program. The second portion of the chapter explains the process of FTP, which is a program used to retrieve files. A brief examination of the different types of files found on the Internet is then provided. The chapter concludes with an explanation of how to find specific files on the Internet via the Archie program.

4.1   TELNET

Telnet is a program that lets you connect (log in) to a remote computer over the Internet. Once you have connected to the remote computer, you can use any resources that are available on that computer just as if you were accessing the resource locally.

Telnet comes in very handy if you are traveling and need access to your computer back at home, work, or school. You simply connect locally to the Internet and use telnet to make the connection to your remote computer. Another advantage of using telnet is that it allows you to connect to several remote computers at the same time (or the same computer multiple times) and do different sets of work simultaneously.

Telnet is a text-based program. When you use telnet, you cannot see any neat graphics or fancy interfaces. When logging in, you may be asked to specify a terminal type. The common types are ANSI, TTY and VT100. ANSI supports color; TTY, is a very plain terminal; VT100 is an old DEC-terminal type and is probably both the most common and most widely used choice.

4.1.1   How Do I Telnet?

Telnet is available on most computers. To use it, you usually must start by typing:

```
Telnet hostname [port]
```

or

```
Telnet IPaddress [port]
```

When connecting to telnet, you can use either the hostname or the IP address since they both represent the same computer. After you have entered the command to start a session, telnet tries to connect to the remote computer. If it is successful, you will be prompted for your username and password.

Occasionally you may need to specify a *port* number. Most of the time, we can just type the telnet command, which automatically connects us to the telnet port on the remote computer. The telnet port allows us to log in to the computer. There are instances, though, when we do not want to connect to the telnet port, but rather to a specific port. For such a case, we would supply the port number after the hostname or IP address. We saw an example of this situation in Chapter 2 when we telneted to the KIS server at Reston. The command was telnet nri.reston.va.us 185. 185 is a port which, when we connect to it, supplies us with the Knowbot Information Service (KIS).

Telnet may not always be able to make the connection that you request. There are primarily three reasons that you might not be able to get to the host you specified:

- You misspelled the hostname.
- The host computer is down.
- The host computer is not connected to the Internet.

The second method to access Telnet is just to type the command *telnet*. You will then receive a Telnet> prompt, from where you can issue the following telnet commands:

?	print help information
close	stop communications with the remote computer
display	display operating parameters
mode	try to enter line-by-line or character-by-character mode
open *host*	attempt to start communications with a remote computer
quit	end the telnet program
send	transmit special characters (type 'help send?' for more information)
set	set operating parameters (type 'help set?' for more information)
status	print status information
toggle	toggle operating parameters (type 'help toggle? for more information)
z	suspend telnet

You also should be aware of what you can do by pressing CTRL-]. This keystroke interrupts your session with the remote computer and returns you to the Telnet> prompt. At that point, you can issue the *quit* command to stop communications with the remote computer and end your telnet session.

4.1.2 An Example of Using Telnet

In this example, I am going to log in to a computer that is physically housed two floors below the computer I am currently using. I could just as easily be accessing a computer halfway around the world.

```
defiant{sjames}10% Telnet markviii.cimlab.kettering.edu
Trying 192.138.137.41 ...
Connected to markviii.cimlab.kettering.edu.
Escape character is '^]'.
```

At this point, I have made the connection and can now attempt to enter my username and password to log in to the computer:

```
*****************************************************************
* Unauthorized Access to this computer system or any information *
*         contained therein is a violation of federal law.       *
*****************************************************************

SunOS UNIX (markviii)

login: sjames
Password:
Last login: Tue May 23 09:46:22 from nova.kettering.edu
SunOS Release 4.1.3_U1 (MARKVIII) #1: Fri Oct 21 16:34:40 EDT 1994
You have new mail.
```

I am remotely connected to the computer and can issue any command that could be issued if I was actually sitting at that computer.

```
markviii{sjames}1% from

From aleonard Thu Apr 27 13:11:12 1996
From cjames Tue May 16 18:13:18 1996
```

```
From hjames Wed May 17 12:01:23 1996

markviii{sjames}2% lpr -Pcimsparc todolist.txt
```

The command I just made is a UNIX command that prints out a specified file. I can now walk downstairs to find that my file has been printed on the remote printer that I specified. One of the greatest advantages of telnet is that I can use my computer from my office at work, my office at home, or anywhere else in the world on the Internet!

4.1.3 Some Telnet Sites to Practice with

If you do not have a remote computer to which to Telnet, here are a few places on the Internet to try. Notice that some of the names also require a port number. If a username is required, it is put in parentheses. These sites are

access.usask.ca (hytelnet)	Online libraries
astro.temple.edu 12345	Quotation cookie server
columbia.ilc.com (cas)	CDs, videotapes and software
cs.indiana.edu 2627 (webster)	Online Webster's dictionary
culine.colorado.edu 862	Today's baseball schedule
downwind.sprl.umich.edu 3000	Weather information
fdabbs.fda.gov (bbs)	FDA database
fedix.fie.com (fedix)	Federal hiring information
fedix.fie.com (molis)	Minority college information
glis.cr.usgs.gov (guest)	Global land usage
hpcvbbs.cv.hp.com	HP calculators
india.colorado.edu 13	MST from an atomic clock
locis.loc.gov	Library of Congress
martini.eecs.umich.edu 3000	Geographic information
pac.carl.org	Colorado Alliance of Research Libraries
ucsdbkst.ucsd.edu	Univeristy of California at San Diego's bookstore

Although it is not an adequate site to practice with, CompuServe can be reached over the Internet if you telnet to *compuserve.com*. When you see the hostname prompt, type *CIS*. You will then get a short disclaimer on usage of CompuServe. (You can type CISAGREE at the hostname prompt to avoid the disclaimer.) You can then type *logon* and select the baud rate. (Remember that the higher the baud rate, the faster the data flow and the more money you pay to CompuServe.) Finally, you will be prompted for your CompuServe User ID and password.

PRACTICE!

Let us practice our telnet skills by finding out the population of Flint, Michigan. To do so, I telnet to the geographic information database stored at *martini.eecs.umich.edu 3000* (the bold text indicates what I type):

```
telnet martini.eecs.umich.edu 3000
Trying 141.213.11.44 ...
Connected to martini.eecs.umich.edu.
Escape character is '^]'.
# Geographic Name Server, Copyright 1992 Regents of the Uni-
versity of Michigan.
# Version 8/19/92.  Use "help" or "?" for assistance, "info"
for hints.
```

The easiest way to use this system is to type the zip code of the location in which you are interested. If you want a full set of instructions, type *help* or ?.

```
48504
0 Northwest
1 26049 Genesee
2 MI Michigan
3 US United States
F 45 Populated place
Z 48504 48531 48532

0 Flint
1 26049 Genesee
2 MI Michigan
3 US United States
R county seat
F 45 Populated place
L 43 00 45 N  83 41 15 W
P 159611
E 712
Z 48500 48501 48502 48503 48504 48505 48506 48507 48508 48509
Z 48529 48531 48532 48550 48551 48552 48553 48554 48555 48556
Z 48559
```

From the information returned, you can see that the population 'P' is 159,611. I can now type *quit* to leave the system, since I have the information for which I was looking. Try it for your city!

4.2 ALTERNATIVE WAYS OF TELNETING

What happens when you need to telnet to a site that interests you, but you do not have local telnet access?

4.2.1 Gopher

Often when you are using gopher, you will receive a message that contains the hostname and/or IP address of the computer to which you are connecting. You should write this information down so that you can telnet directly to the host without having to go through the gopher menus every time. You should know that some of the support that gopher supplies is in the form of a telnet session; therefore, gopher has telnet service built into itself. Thus, In the future, you can start gopher with the address of the computer to which you want to telnet, thereby gaining access to it. Gopher is examined in Chapter 5.

4.2.2 Web Browsers

Most Web browsers allow you to perform a telnet session by typing *telnet://hostname* in the browser's URL line. Web browsers are examined in Chapter 6.

4.3 FTP

FTP stands for File Transfer Protocol and is a mechanism for transferring files between two computers. FTP, like telnet is one of the oldest TCP/IP protocols still around. It is very simple to use and effective in what it does. FTP allows you to transfer both binary and text files. Be aware, however, that FTP is case sensitive for both files and commands.

Why use FTP?

- It is a quick and painless way to transfer files from home to work or school and vice versa.
- You can use it to transfer data files from the Internet to your own computer.
- There is enough free software on the Internet to last a lifetime for every computer system imaginable, and FTP is one of the most common ways to download it. A list of publicly accessible FTP sites is downloadable via anonymous FTP from *pilot.njin.net* in the */pub/ftp-list/* directory.

4.3.1 How Do I Use FTP?

Because FTP and telnet are old TCP/IP programs, both have the same operating mechanics. We can start an FTP session by typing

```
ftp hostname
```

or

```
ftp IPaddress
```

or

```
ftp
```

which gets you an `ftp>` prompt, after which you type

```
open hostname
```

FTP then attempts to connect you to the specified host. If it is successful, you will be prompted to log in. If the computer to which you have FTPed is a private FTP server, you will probably need to have an account on that computer in order to access it. If the FTP server is a public server, you can usually log in by typing *anonymous* for the username and your full electronic address for the password.

If you can not connect to a given FTP site and the FTP server is a public server, you may be shown a list of mirror sites to which you could try to FTP. A mirror site is a site that carries an exact copy of the what is on the computer you were trying to reach.

The FTP commands that you typically use during a session are:

ascii	States that you are going to perform an access in text mode
bin	States that you are going to perform an access in binary mode
bye	Logs out of the FTP computer
cd	Changes directory on the FTP computer

dir	Lists files and their related information, such as size, date created, etc.
get *file*	Downloads a file from the FTP computer to your computer
hash	Displays # marks while files are being transferred
help	Gives a list of commands
lcd	Change directory on the local machine
ls	Lists files in the current directory
mget *file*	Downloads multiple files from the FTP computer to your computer
mput *file*	Uploads multiple files from your computer to the FTP computer
prompt	Toggles prompt mode for mget or mput operations
put file	Uploads a file from your computer to the FTP computer

Note that get and mget automatically overwrite any local files with the same name.

APPLICATION:
USING FTP TO COPY APPLICATIONS FROM THE INTERNET

Suppose that, I am at a client's business at which there are no virus scanners in use on any of the computers. Since there are a lot of good free or cheap virus scanners on the Internet, I will download one. I am going to FTP to a computer at Oakland University, located in Rochester, Michigan, and download a copy of the MS-DOS antivirus package, F-PROT. I begin by invoking the FTP command for the computer to which I want to connect at Oakland:

```
nova{sjames}5% ftp oak.oakland.edu
Connected to oak.oakland.edu.
220 oak.oakland.edu FTP server (Version wu-2.4(9) Wed May 3 15:02:49 EDT 1995)
ready.
```

At this point, I am connected to the computer at Oakland, and my username and password will be requested. I will type in *anonymous* for the username and *sjames@defiant.kettering.edu* for the password. Since Oakland is a public FTP site, I should not have any problems with this procedure.

```
Name (oak.oakland.edu:sjames): anonymous
331 Guest login ok, send your complete e-mail address as password.
Password:
230-
230-                          Welcome to
230-                THE OAK SOFTWARE REPOSITORY
230-      A service of Oakland University, Rochester Michigan
230-
230- If you have trouble using OAK with your ftp client, please try using
230- a dash (-) as the first character of your password -- this will turn
230- off the continuation messages that may be confusing your ftp client.
230- OAK is a Unix machine, and filenames are case sensitive.
230-
230- Access is allowed at any time.  If you have any unusual problems,
230- please report them via electronic mail to archives@Oakland.Edu
230-
230- Oak is also on the World Wide Web, URL: http://www.acs.oakland.edu/oak.html
```

```
230-
230- File searching is now available!  Example command:  site exec index 4dos
230-
230-Please read the file README
230-  it was last modified on Fri Mar 24 18:59:19 1995 - 61 days ago
230 Guest login ok, access restrictions apply.
```

I'm now logged into the computer. Let's take a look around:

```
ftp> dir
200 PORT command successful.
150 Opening ASCII mode data connection for /bin/ls.
total 1258
-rw-r--r--   1 w8sdz     OAK             0 Nov 13  1994 .notar
drwxr-x---   2 root      operator     8192 Dec 31 16:44 .quotas
drwx------   2 root      system       8192 Dec 30 19:16 .tags
-rw-r--r--   1 jeff      OAK       1093470 May 24 03:20 Index-byname
-r--r--r--   1 w8sdz     OAK          1237 Mar 24 18:59 README
drwxr-xr-x   3 w8sdz     OAK          8192 May 19 17:53 SimTel
d--x--x--x   3 root      system       8192 Jan 19 20:26 bin
d--x--x--x   2 root      system       8192 Jul 30  1994 core
drwxr-x---   2 cpm       OAK          8192 Nov 21  1994 cpm-incoming
d--x--x--x   5 root      system       8192 Dec 30 05:15 etc
drwxrwx---   2 incoming  OAK          8192 May 24 11:54 incoming
drwxrwx---   2 25913     OAK          8192 Apr 23 10:50 nt-incoming
drwxr-xr-x   3 w8sdz     OAK          8192 Apr 13 19:46 pub
drwxr-xr-x  15 w8sdz     OAK          8192 Apr 13 19:46 pub2
drwxr-xr-x   8 w8sdz     OAK          8192 May  3 13:24 pub3
drwxr-xr-x   3 w8sdz     OAK          8192 May 19 17:53 simtel
drwxr-xr-x   2 jeff      OAK          8192 Apr 17  1994 siteinfo
drwx------  46 w8sdz     OAK          8192 May 22 21:42 w8sdz
226 Transfer complete.
1133 bytes received in 0.45 seconds (2.5 Kbytes/s)
```

I happen to know that the MS-DOS programs are located in the SimTel directory, so let's change directories.

```
ftp> cd SimTel
250-The files in this directory tree are a mirror of SimTel, the Coast to
250-Coast Software Repository (tm).  Please read README.COPYRIGHT for
250-information on distribution rights.
250-
250-Please read the file README.COPYRIGHT
250-  it was last modified on Sun Apr 23 01:32:42 1995 - 31 days ago
250-Please read the file README.MIRRORING
250-  it was last modified on Thu Apr 27 12:49:22 1995 - 27 days ago
250 CWD command successful.
```

There's the msdos directory. Let's change there:

```
ftp> dir
200 PORT command successful.
150 Opening ASCII mode data connection for /bin/ls.
total 32
-rw-r--r--   1 w8sdz     OAK           172 Jan 28 15:05 .message
-rw-r--r--   1 w8sdz     OAK             0 Jan 28 15:05 .notar
```

```
-rw-r--r--   3 w8sdz     OAK       4605 Apr 23 01:32 README.COPYRIGHT
-rw-r--r--   3 w8sdz     OAK       1632 Apr 27 12:49 README.MIRRORING
drwxr-xr-x 221 w8sdz     OAK       8192 May 22 01:27 msdos
drwxr-xr-x  11 djgruber  OAK       8192 May 20 02:57 nt
drwxr-xr-x  84 w8sdz     OAK       8192 May 23 23:21 win3
226 Transfer complete.
459 bytes received in 0.011 seconds (41 Kbytes/s)
ftp> cd msdos
250-This MS-DOS collection is a mirror of SimTel, the Coast to Coast
250-Software Repository (tm).  Questions about or comments on this
250-collection should be sent to w8sdz@SimTel.Coast.NET.
250-
250-Please read the file README.COPYRIGHT
250-  it was last modified on Sun Apr 23 01:32:42 1995 - 31 days ago
250-Please read the file README.MIRRORING
250-  it was last modified on Thu Apr 27 12:49:22 1995 - 27 days ago
250-Please read the file README.descriptions
250-  it was last modified on Sun Apr 23 01:38:53 1995 - 31 days ago
250-Please read the file README.dir-list
250-  it was last modified on Mon May 22 01:24:32 1995 - 2 days ago
250-Please read the file README.file-formats
250-  it was last modified on Sun Apr 23 01:40:24 1995 - 31 days ago
250-Please read the file README.how-to-upload
250-  it was last modified on Sun Apr 23 01:35:51 1995 - 31 days ago
250-Please read the file README.simtel-cdrom
250-  it was last modified on Fri May 12 12:36:58 1995 - 12 days ago
250 CWD command successful.
```

The msdos directory is huge; it probably has a couple hundred subdirectories. I know that the name of the subdirectory for which I am looking is "virus." I now change to that subdirectory:

```
ftp> cd virus
250 CWD command successful.
```

Let us look for any files that start with fp:

```
ftp> dir fp*.*
200 PORT command successful.
150 Opening ASCII mode data connection for /bin/ls.
-rw-r--r--   1 w8sdz     OAK        564320 Apr  2 16:04 fp-217.zip
226 Transfer complete.
remote: fp*.*
66 bytes received in 0.0051 seconds (13 Kbytes/s)
```

I have found the file that I want to download. It is a binary file; I know this because the file was found in the binary directory, /bin and because its file extension (.zip) is a type of binary file extension, which we will learn more about in Section 4.4. So, we change into binary mode and download the file:

```
ftp> bin
200 Type set to I.
ftp> get fp-217.zip
200 PORT command successful.
150 Opening BINARY mode data connection for fp-217.zip (564320 bytes).
226 Transfer complete.
local: fp-217.zip remote: fp-217.zip
564320 bytes received in 92 seconds (6 Kbytes/s)
```

I just downloaded half a megabyte in 92 seconds. I now have a copy of the F-PROT program on my computer. I can now exit the FTP program.

```
ftp> quit
221 Goodbye.
```

I can now install the file onto my client's computer system. Once again, immediate access to software via the Internet has proved useful.

4.3.2 Sample FTP Sites to Start with

The following list contains some FTP sites that you may want to try out to practice using FTP:

ames.arc.nasa.gov	NASA files and images
cathouse.org	Entertainment information
explorer.arc.nasa.gov	NASA Explorer
ftp.cica.indiana.edu	Windows software
ftp.fedworld.gov	Helps you find federal government documents
ftp.microsoft.com	Microsoft's FTP site
ftp.ncsa.uiuc.edu	Incomplete Guide to the Internet
ftp.near.net	Commerce Business Daily
ftp.product.com	Provider of product information
ftp.senate.gov	U.S. Senate
ftp.uu.net	Amiga and Macintosh files
marvel.loc.gov	Library of Congress
mrcnext.cso.uiuc.edu	Project Gutenberg
oak.oakland.edu	A SimTel site with a lot of everything
stats.bls.gov	Bureau of Labor Statistics
sunsite.unc.edu	Internet tools and Sun information
wiretap.spies.com	FOIA home containing a lot of information
wuarchive.wustl.edu	Washington University at St. Louis site *SimTel mirror*

PRACTICE!

Let us try to FTP the file called README from the FTP site *oak.oakland.edu*. You need to connect as user *anonymous* and type your username for the password (The bold text indicates what I typed):

```
ftp oak.oakland.edu
Connected to oak.oakland.edu.
220 oak.oakland.edu FTP server (Version wu-2.4(9) Wed May 3 15:02:49 EDT
1995) r
eady.
Name (oak.oakland.edu:sjames): anonymous
331 Guest login ok, send your complete e-mail address as password.
Password:
230-
230-                              Welcome to
230-                    THE OAK SOFTWARE REPOSITORY
230-          A service of Oakland University, Rochester Michigan
```

```
230- If you have trouble using OAK with your ftp client, please try using
230- a dash (-) as the first character of your password -- this will turn
230- off the continuation messages that may be confusing your ftp client.
230- OAK is a Unix machine, and filenames are case sensitive.
230-
230- Access is allowed at any time.  If you have any unusual problems,
230- please report them via electronic mail to archives@Oakland.Edu
230-
230- Oak is also on the World Wide Web, URL: http://oak.oakland.edu/
230-
230- To search for files, use the command: quote site exec index filename
230-
230-Please read the file README
230-  it was last modified on Fri Mar 22 15:07:51 1996 - 146 days ago
230 Guest login ok, access restrictions apply.
```

Now that we are on the system, let's look around:

```
ftp>dir
200 PORT command successful.
150 Opening ASCII mode data connection for /bin/ls.
total 1874
-rw-r--r--    1 w8sdz    OAK            0 Nov 13  1994 .notar
drwxr-x---    2 root     operator    8192 Dec 31  1994 .quotas
drwx------    2 root     system      8192 Dec 30  1994 .tags
-rw-r--r--    1 jeff     OAK      1826389 Aug 15 03:19 Index-byname
-r--r--r--    1 w8sdz    OAK         1386 Mar 22 15:07 README
drwxr-xr-x    2 jeff     OAK         8192 Apr 28 22:21 SimTel
d--x--x--x    3 root     system      8192 Jan 19  1995 bin
d--x--x--x    2 root     system      8192 May  6 16:11 core
drwxr-x---    3 cpm      OAK         8192 Mar 22 16:46 cpm-incoming
d--x--x--x    6 root     system      8192 Aug 14 03:14 etc
drwxr-xr-x   10 jeff     OAK         8192 Jul 22 08:32 irc
drwxr-xr-x   16 w8sdz    OAK         8192 Jul 24 15:41 pub
drwxr-xr-x    2 jeff     OAK         8192 Apr 17  1994 siteinfo
drwx------   46 w8sdz    OAK         8192 Aug  5 19:48 w8sdz
226 Transfer complete.
879 bytes received in 0.13 seconds (6.6 Kbytes/s)
```

Since we see the file README, we can get it:

```
ftp>get README
200 PORT command successful.
150 Opening ASCII mode data connection for README (1386 bytes).
226 Transfer complete.
local: README remote: README
1415 bytes received in 0.17 seconds (8 Kbytes/s)
```

Now that we have received it, we can type *quit* to stop the FTP program:

```
ftp> quit
221 Goodbye.
```

If you look at your local disk now, you should see that you have a copy of the README file on it.

4.4 WHAT DO ALL THE FILE EXTENSIONS MEAN?

This section is designed to point out the common file extensions and the program that produced them. If you are trying to download a file in the *binary files* section, make sure that you type the bin command before you try to get the file. Most of the time when we are accessing binary files via FTP they are *compressed* or *archived*. The following list of binary file extensions includes the programs needed to decompress or unarchive some of these files:

Binary Files

.au	Sun Audio files
.bmp	Graphics/Image files
.com	PC executables (programs)
.exe	PC executables (programs)
.gif	Graphics/Image files
.gl	Graphics/Image files
.gz	GNU ZIP file. Use gunzip or gzip -d to extract the files.
.hqx	Macintosh BINHEX file. Use unhqx to extract the files.
.jpg	Graphics/Image files
.lha	LH archive. Use lharc to extract the files.
.mpg	Graphics/Image files
.pcx	Graphics/Image files
.qt	Macintosh QuickTime movie format
.shar	Shell archive. Use unshar to extract the files.
.sit	Macintosh StuffIt format. Use unstuffit to extract the files.
.tar	UNIX tape archive file. Use tar -xvf to extract the files.
.tif	Graphics/Image files
.wav	Windows Audio files
.Z or .z	UNIX compress file. Use uncompress to extract the files.
.zip	ZIP file. Use pkunzip to unzip the files.
.zoo	ZOO archive. Use zoo -extract to extract the files.

Text Files

.me	Readme files
.ps	Postscript files
.txt	Text files
.uue	uuencoded files

When you begin FTPing, you should always start looking at files called README, Index, and so forth. These files give you information about what may be contained in a directory. You can usually view a text file directly on the screen by issuing the command get *filename* |more. There should be no space between the | and the command *more*.

If you download a file that has been compressed, you will need to uncompress it before you can use it. Many sites to which you FTP will have a directory which contains the appropriate program to decompress the files. You may need to look around a bit, but you should be able to find the program.

4.5 ALTERNATIVE WAYS OF FTPING

This section addresses ways to FTP files using e-mail when you do not have access to FTP. One site that e-mails files to you is *ftpmail.decwrl.dec.com*. To perform the FTP download via e-mail, send a message to the server with the FTP commands that you would type if you were manually FTPing in the body of the message. Valid FTP commands include ascii, binary, get, dir, ls, help, quit, and

reply *yourfulladdress*	tells the server where to mail the files
connect *host*	the host where the files are
chdir	change directory

An example of the use of this method is as follows:

```
To:   ftpmail@decwrl.dec.com
Subject:
Message:    reply sjames@nova.kettering.edu
            connect oak.oakland.edu
            chdir /SimTel/msdos/virus
            get fp-217.zip
            quit
```

If the file that you request is larger than 64K, ftpmail will break it up into several numbered sections that you will have to put back together using your computer's particular operating system.

Here is a list of other ftpmail servers around the world, along with their IP addresses and locations:

ftpmail@grasp.insa-lyon.fr	134.214.100.25	France
bitftp@vm.grd.de	192.88.97.13	Germany
ftpmail@ieunet.ie	192.111.39.1	Ireland
ftpmail@decwrl.dec.com	16.1.0.1	USA: California
bitftp@pucc.princeton.edu	128.112.129.99	USA: New Jersey

4.6 HOW CAN I FIND FILES?

Locating files on the Internet that can be obtained via FTP is made possible through a program known as *Archie*. Archie is accessible in three different ways:

1. You could telnet to an Archie server.
2. You could have your own Archie program.
3. You could e-mail an Archie server with a query so that the server e-mails its results back to you.

Let us examine each of these options.

We could begin by telneting to *archie.rutgers.edu* and logging in with the username of *archie*; no password is required. A list of public Archie servers is provided at the end of this chapter.

We now receive an `archie>` prompt. At this point, we can enter search commands; *help* will provide help and *quit* will end our use of the server.

We should now set our search variables. The command *show* will show the values or levels to which all variables are currently set. You can also type *show variable* to find out the value of a particular variable. Let us look at these variables and their associated values:

Environment Variables

set pager [on | off]	You should set pager to on if you want Archie to display its search results to your screen. It causes the results to pause after a full page has been displayed.
set status [on | off]	Set status to on if you want Archie to display a status line at the bottom of the screen as it searches.
set autologout [x]	This value controls how many minutes Archie will wait for you to enter a command without logging you off (range is 1 - 300).
set maxhits [x]	This value tells Archie to stop searching if it finds the same file *x* times. (Start at 10 and move up as needed.)
set mailto *fullusername*	If you want Archie to mail its results to you, you should set this variable to your *username@host.name* information.

Output Density Variables

set output_format verbose	Give as much information as possible
set output_format terse	Give basic information
set output_format machine	Used to specify a program to manipulate the mailed output

Sorting Variables

set sortby none	Do not sort
set sortby filename	Sort alphabetically by filename
set sortby hostname	Sort alphabetically by hostname
set sortby size	Sort largest to smallest
set sortby time	Sort newest to oldest
set sortby rfilename	Reverse-sort alphabetically by filename
set sortby rhostname	Reverse-sort alphabetically by hostname
set sortby rsize	Sort smallest to largest
set sortby rtime	Sort oldest to newest

Searching Variables

set search exact	Searches for the *exact* keyword you type in, operating on a case-sensitive basis. For example, the command "find IBM-PC" returns matches for IBM-PC, but not IBM-pc or ibm-pc.

set search sub	Searches for filenames that contain the keyword you type in, but is not case-sensitive. For example, the command "find PC" returns matches for IBM-PC, PC, or pc-DOS.
set search subcase	Searches for filenames that contain the keyword you type in and is case-sensitive. For example, the command "find PC" matches for IBM-PC, but not pc-DOS.
set search regex	UNIX regular expression that searches for filenames that contain all or part of the keyword you type in in the manner you indicate with a meta-character. (See the next two sections on metacharacters.) For example, the command "findPC$" returns anything ending with the letters PC.
set search exact_sub	First runs an exact search, then runs a sub search.
set search exact_subcase	First runs an exact search, then runs a subcase search.
set search exact_regex	First runs an exact search, then runs a regex search.

Metacharacters

The main expression metacharacters for use in a regex search are:

$ indicates "ending with"; "find PC$" finds anything ending with PC.

^   indicates "beginning with"; "find ^pkunzip" finds anything starting with pkunzip.

.   matches any character.

*   matches zero or more preceding characters

[ ]   matches one of the characters contained within the brackets.

Examples of Metacharacter Matches

Pattern	What does it match?
bag	bag
^bag	bag, baggage
bag$	old-bag
^bag$	bag
[Bb]ag	Bag, bag
b[aeiou]g	bag,beg,big,bog,bug
b.g	b anything for the second character g
^...$	anyline with exactly three characters
bugs*	bug,bugs,bugss,etc.
"word"	a word that is enclosed within quotation marks
"*word"*	a word that may or may not be enclosed within quotation marks

The last command that we need to supply is *find filename,* which tells Archie to look for a file with the supplied name. In older versions of Archie, this command was called *prog.*

4.6.1 A Sample Archie Search

The following example illustrates a search we might make using Archie:

```
Archie> set maxhits 10
Archie> set output_format verbose
Archie> set pager
Archie> set search exact_sub
Archie> set sortby time
Archie> set status
Archie> find fp-217.zip
```

After receiving these commands, Archie tries to locate the file *fp-217.zip*. If you want Archie to stop before it finishes searching, press the CTRL-C combination. Once Archie has completed a search, you can e-mail the results to yourself by entering the command *mail*, given that you have set the *mailto* variable. Otherwise, you must type *mail yourfulladdress*. So in this example, I could type the following command to mail my results as soon as I get the `Archie>` prompt back:

```
Archie> mail sjames@defiant.kettering.edu
```

There are a few keystrokes that are convenient to know when looking at the search results displayed on the computer screen. The *space* key moves forward one full screen; *q* quits displaying the output; *b* goes backward one full screen; */pattern* searches forward for the given pattern (you can use *?pattern* to search backwards); and *n* repeats the previous search.

The *find* command is useful if you know the name of the file for which you are searching, but what if you only know part of the name, or worse yet, none of it? The *whatis* command is helpful in such a situation. If you simply type *whatis itemtosearch-for*, *whatis* returns anything with a description containing that item. The only limitation on *whatis* is that the person who submitted the file to the Archie database must have supplied a description that contains your search word in it; otherwise, you will not receive information about the file in your search results.

Archie also has a help function. *Help ?* brings up a list of all commands, and *help command* brings up detailed help on the specified command. The same keystrokes mentioned previously for viewing the output generated by Archie will work with help too.

The second way that you may be able to access Archie is on your local computer. Try typing `archie` and see if you get the `archie>` prompt. The way this version of Archie works is a little different from telnetting to an Archie server. You will not need to set variables as in the previous sample search, and the entire command will fit on one line. For example, `archie -m10 -s fp-217.zip` tells the computer to set the maxhits variable to 10 and to use a sub search look for the file fp-217.zip, sending the output to your screen. All the commands are typically switches that are supplied on the command line. They are:

-c	set search subcase
-e	set search exact
-h*address*	send Archie server requests to the specified host
-l	set output_format machine
-L	show list of known Archie servers
-m*number*	set maxhits
-o*filename*	send the output to the specified file

-r	set search regex
-s	set search sub
-t	set sortby time
-V	provides feedback during a long search

Finally, you can search Archie through e-mail by sending a message to *archie@archie.internic.net* or *archie@archie.mcgill.ca*. To do so, type a text message with each of the variables and commands that you would normally type if you were performing an Archie search via a telnet session. These commands should be in the body of the message, and the subject line of the message should be blank.

If you would like to receive information on how to use the Archie e-mail service, send a message with the word *help* as the body of the message; leave the subject line blank. A sample Archie search as conducted through e-mail is as follows:

```
To:      archie@archie.internic.net
Subject:
Message:     set mailto sjames@nova.kettering.edu
             set maxhits 25
             set output_format verbose
             set search exact
             set sortby time
             find fp-217.zip
             quit
```

4.6.2 A List of Publicly Available Archie Servers in the U.S. and Canada

archie.uqam.ca	Canada
archie.mcgill.ca	Canada
archie.sura.net	U.S.: Maryland
archie.unl.edu	U.S.: Nebraska
archie.internic.net	U.S.: New Jersey
archie.rutgers.edu	U.S.: New Jersey
archie.ans.net	U.S.: New York

SUMMARY

This chapter has looked at two of the oldest communications programs around: telnet and FTP. Telnet provides users with the ability to log on to computers located on the Internet. FTP is a program that allows users to copy files from a remote computer to their own local computer. The chapter has concluded with an examination of how to locate specific filenames on the Internet.

KEY TERMS

Archie	Compressed	Telnet
Archive	FTP	Text Files
Binary Files	Port	

Problems

1. Practice telneting to computers that are located on your school's campus.
2. Telnet to *downwind.sprl.umich.edu 3000* and print out the weather forecast for your vicinity.

3. Telnet to *martini.eecs.umich.edu 3000* and print out the geographic information for your hometown. (Remember to use your zip code.)

4. Retrieve a text file via FTP from a computer of your instructor's choice. Print out that file.

5. FTP the lastest version of the MS-DOS antivirus package F-PROT. You can get it from the */pub/simtelnet/msdos/virus* directory at *oak.oakland.edu*.

6. Use an Archie server to find other Internet sites where the latest version of F-PROT can be found. Print out this list.

5

Gopher and WAIS

SCIENCE/ENGINEERING SPOTLIGHT: VIRTUAL REALITY

We have all seen people playing the games in which contestants put on headsets and gloves and try to "zap" each other with lasers while trying not to become a pterodactyl snack. We have also seen movies like *The Lawnmower Man* and *Virtuosity*, which depict virtual worlds. Where does virtual reality currently exist, though? Virtual reality is still in a stage of infancy, such that most participants must wear goggles or a headset in order to see and hear the virtual world. If one wants to manipulate items in the virtual world, a special glove apparatus is required. We are making advances in our pursuits to enable people to become immersed in the technology through the use of special suits that provide tactile feedback. The truth of the matter is that we are still a long way from VR as it is depicted in movies.

SECTIONS

OBJECTIVES

After reading this chapter, you should be able to:

- Explain what Gopher, Veronica, and Jughead are
- Know what WAIS is, and what is replacing it

57

This chapter examines the last two of the text-based services on the Internet. Gophers are a menu-driven approach to integrating the collection of data resources pooled through telneting and FTPing. Gopher is actually a forerunner of Web browsers, which will be examined in Chapter 6. WAIS is a collection of databases that users can select to perform searches on. Any matches found in the databases can immediately be retrieved from the WAIS interface.

5.1 GOPHER

Gopher integrates the different tasks performed by the numerous different Internet services we have examined into a common text-based environment. Gopher is a menu-driven system that allows users to have access to different resources at sites across the Internet. You do not even need to know exactly where something is stored before you try to find it. You only need to set your gopher software to point at any gopher server. Basically, if you can use a table of contents in a book, you can use gopher to move throughout the Internet to retrieve the information that you want.

5.1.1 Gopher-Related Terms

The following is a list of terms that are commonly found when you use a Gopher:

- *Item:* Any item that appears on a menu: it could be another menu, a directory, document or a search.
- *Document:* the actual object associated with an item. It is usually text, but objects can come in other forms as well.
- *Gopherspace:* the total of all gopher resources on the Internet.
- *Server:* a computer system that provides the gopher's menus and stores the related documents.

5.1.2 How Do I Use Gopher?

You must have some form of gopher software in order to use gopher. You need only point that software at a gopher server. Everything on gopher is menu driven. Gopher software is truly of a client/server in nature. The *client* portion is the program that resides on your computer, and the *server* portion is the set of actual documents and menus that exist on gopher servers.

The newer versions of gopher are starting to blur with the World Wide Web in that gopher is no longer exclusively text based. Audio files, graphic images, and animations are just a few of the documents that are retrievable and viewable with the newer versions of gopher software.

5.1.3 An Example of the Use of Gopher

I begin this example by starting the local gopher program on my computer at Kettering:

```
nova{sjames}4% gopher
Welcome to the wonderful world of Gopher!

Gopher has limitations on its use and comes without
a warranty.  Please refer to the file 'Copyright' included
in the distribution.

Internet Gopher Information Client 2.0 patch16
```

```
Copyright 1991,92,93,94 by the Regents of the University of
Minnesota

Press RETURN to continue
```

Now that I am running gopher, I can press the return key to bring up the main menu:

```
Kettering Gopher Information Server Main Menu

 --> 1.  About This Gopher at KETTERING(Updated 3/5/95)
     2.  The KETTERING Undergraduate Catalog - 1994-1995 <HTML>
     3.  Academic Programs/
     4.  CSO Version of the KETTERING Phonebook <CSO>
     5.  Unix Update - KETTERING/
     6.  Calendars and Schedules/
     7.  Computer Policy at KETTERING/
     8.  Computer Resources at KETTERING(lots of help)/
     9.  KETTERING Campus Organizations and People/
    10.  KETTERING Falcon Library Catalog <TEL>
    11.  General Interest - Non-Kettering/
    12.  Scholarly and Academic Resources/
    13.  Virtual Visitors' Center/
    14.  Select this if using a WWW browser and you opened gopher:


Press ? for Help, q to Quit
```

Notice that the last line on the screen shows you how to get help and how to quit. Gopher is very user friendly in that each screen always presents you with options.

The other item of importance is the → in front of option 1. This set of characters is my pointer and I can move it by pressing the up and down arrows. If I want to enter a menu option, I can press the right arrow to select it or the left arrow to unselect it.

A slash (/) after a particular menu option indicates that there are submenu choices under it. Let us choose option 11 (I can just type in the 11 rather than pressing the down arrow until the pointer reaches option 11):

```
General Interest - Non-Kettering

 --> 1.  Auroral Activity
     2.  Computer Software Archives/
     3.  Current Events/
     4.  Education/
     5.  Entertainment/
     6.  Flint Computer Resources - GFEC Hypertext Page <HTML>
     7.  Flint Local Weather Forecast
     8.  General Weather Forecast/
     9.  Libraries/
    10.  Miscellaneous Network Services/
    11.  Newspapers and Newsmagazines/
    12.  Online Books and Journals/
    13.  Other gophers/
    14.  Politics/
```

I now have another set of choices. Let us look at choice 12, "Online Books and Journals," which, also has submenu choices.

```
Online Books and Journals

  -->  1. Voice of America and Worldnet Television/
       2. A Collection on College Campus Newspapers <HTML>
       3. ACADEME THIS WEEK (Chronicle of Higher Education)/
       4. Annals of Improbable Research(also J.of Irreproducble
          Results)/
       5. Classics Collections (wiretap.spies.com)/
       6. Computer-Mediated Communication Magazine <HTML>
       7. EDUCOM Documents and News/
       8. Electric Mystics Guide/
       9. Electronic Journals/
       10.Electronic Publications and Resources/
       11.GTOnline from the Colorado City Gazette Telegraph <HTML>
       12.Journals at University of Michigan Library/
       13.Learned NewsWire 1.5 <HTML>
       14.On-Line College Papers (LA Tech Gopher)/
       15.Project Gutenberg/
       16.The Interpedia Project/
       17.Time-Warner Publications Online <HTML>
       18.WIRED Magazine/
```

From here I can enter a host of other choices, such as 15, "Project Gutenberg," which is responsible for taking literature and converting it into an online electronic version. books from the CIA World Factbook to the King James Version of the Bible can be found there.

There are a few public gopher clients that you can access via telnet. Here is a list of the public clients in the U.S., listed by state:

State	Hostname	Login as
CA	*gopher.ora.com*	gopher
CA	*infopath.ucsd.edu*	infopath
CA	*infoslug.ucsc.edu*	infoslug
CA	*scilibx.ucsc.edu*	gopher
GA	*grits.valdosta.peachnet.edu*	gopher
IL	*gopher.uiuc.edu*	gopher
IL	*ux1.cso.uiuc.edu*	gopher
IA	*panda.uiowa.edu*	panda
MD	*inform.umd.edu*	gopher
MD	*seymour.md.gov*	gopher
MI	*gopher.msu.edu*	gopher
MN	*consultant.micro.umn.edu*	gopher
NC	*gopher.unc.edu*	gopher
NC	*sunsite.unc.edu*	gopher
NC	*twosocks.ces.ncsu.edu*	gopher
OH	*gopher.ohiolink.edu*	gopher
VA	*ecosys.drdr.virginia.edu*	gopher
VA	*gopher.virginia.edu*	gwis
WI	*wsuaix.csc.wsu.edu*	wsuinfo
WI	*telnet.wiscinfo.wisc.edu*	wiscinfo

As previously mentioned, moving around in the original text-based version of gopher is easy: You use the four *arrow keys* to move up and down menus, select, and deselect; *space* to go to the next page; and *b* to go back a page. If you have any need for help just push the *?* key. To stop your session, press *q* and you will be asked if you want to quit, you can respond *y*(es) or *n*(o). If you want to quit without being asked to verify this choice, press *Q*.

5.1.4 Gopher Server Sites to Start with

Once you have your gopher client software loaded and configured, point it at these server sites to get started:

ashpool.micro.umn.edu	Washington University archive, Internet Resource Guide
boombox.micro.umn.edu	Gopher distribution archive
chaos.taylored.com	Cypherpunks gopher site
dartcms1.dartmouth.edu	Federal job openings
deming.eng.clemson.edu	TQM
english-server.hss.cmu.edu	Wide range of subject matter
eryx.syr.edu	Electronic Government Information Service
garnet.msen.com	Internet Business pages
gopher.bu.edu	Boston metropolitan guide
gopher.concert.net	U of NC archives
gopher.cpsr.com	Computer Professionals for Social Responsibility
gopher.eff.org	EFF archive
gopher.house.gov	U.S. House gopher
gopher.msen.com	Search for individuals on the Internet
gopher.uis.itd.umich.edu	U of M archive
hunter.cs.unr.edu	Search Gopherspace using Veronica
infopath.ucsd.edu	Business statistics
internic.net	Internet directory services (lists of lists & sites)
jupiter.sun.csd.unb.ca	FAQ's from UseNet
marvel.loc.gov	Library of Congress
metaverse.com	Adam Curry's site
obi.std.com	Phone books, BBS listings, etc.
riceinfo.rice.edu	Business and economics repository
una.hh.lib.umich.edu	Economic bulletin board
wiretap.spies.com	Cyberspace, Humor, etc.
wiretap.spies.com	White House press releases
wx.atmos.uiuc.edu	Weather maps

In addition, these U.S. Gopher sites provide some UseNet News access:

Site	**Menu Path**
aurora.latech.edu	/USENET News
gopher.msu.edu	/News & Weather/USENET news
info-server.lanl.gov	/Network News (USENET)
saturn.wwc.edu	/USENET News via gopher

PRACTICE!

> Find out what Gopher resources you have access to and use your local gopher system. If the computers you commonly use don't have a gopher client, download one for your own computer via FTP. After you have a gopher client, point it to one of the public Gopher sites listed above to try out the gopher system.

5.2 USING VERONICA TO SEARCH GOPHERSPACE

Veronica is a Gopher-based resource that you can use to search Gopherspace for menu items that contain words you provide. To start Veronica, you should look for options that say something to the extent of "Search titles in Gopherspace using Veronica" this will often be located under a menu item that says "Other Gopher and Information Services."

You should then be presented with a menu from which you choose where to run Veronica, and after you select one of the provided servers, a dialog box will appear to ask you what to search for. Veronica is not case sensitive in its searches.

Say that we want to find pictures of trees. Initially, we might try to search for <u>trees</u>. Unfortunately, we would find too much information on trees from this search, some of it text based, so we need to narrow down our search using the commands *and* and *or*. So, we could try <u>trees and pictures</u>, which probably would give us a smaller list. We might want to limit our search further by trying the command <u>trees and (pictures or images)</u>.

You probably get the idea. The other command we could include in our search is *not*; for example, we could use the command <u>trees and pictures not wanted</u> to screen out the requests of other people who have requested the same thing we just have. We can also include an asterisk (*) to indicate extra characters at the end of a word—for example, <u>trees and pictures not want*</u>—to avoid finding items with "want," "wanted," and "wanting."

Additionally, you can include a *-t flag* option in the search box to tell Veronica to find only certain document types.

Listing of Veronica Document Types:

0 - Text File	s - Sound
1 - Directory	e - Event
2 - CSO name server	I - Image other than GIF
4 - Mac HQX file	M - MIME message
5 - PC binary	i - Inline text type
6 - UNIX uuencoded file	T - TN3270 session
7 - Full Text Index (Gopher Menu)	c - Calendar
8 - Telnet session	g - GIF image
9 - Binary file	h - HTML

An example of the use of a *-t flag* option is *trees -t g*, which instructs Veronica to search only for GIF images of trees.

APPLICATION:
FINDING ONLINE INFORMATION USING VERONICA

Many times when doing research papers, you have an immediate need for information or statistics. In this example, let us assume I need to know the atomic numbers of some elements. In other words, I need to find an online version of the periodic table. Gopher would probably be an ideal way to find it, but I do not know where a periodic table is located. I begin my search by accessing my gopher software and then pointing at a Veronica search site:

```
Internet Gopher Information Client v2.0.16

                 Other Gopher and Information Servers

         1.  All the Gopher Servers in the World/
         2.  Search All the Gopher Servers in the World <?>
   -->   3.  Search titles in Gopherspace using veronica/
         4.  Africa/
         5.  Asia/
         6.  Europe/
         7.  International Organizations/
         8.  Middle East/
         9.  North America/
        10.  Pacific/
        11.  Russia/
        12.  South America/
        13.  Terminal Based Information/
        14.  WAIS Based Information/
        15.  Gopher Server Registration <??>



Press ? for Help, q to Quit, u to go up a menu            Page: 1/1
```

I notice that option 3 is "Search titles in gopherspace with Veronica." This option sounds like what I am looking for. I then press 3 or the return key to go to the next menu screen:

```
Internet Gopher Information Client v2.0.16

              Search titles in Gopherspace using veronica

         3.  Find GOPHER DIRECTORIES by Title word(s) (via NYSERNet) <?>
         4.  Find GOPHER DIRECTORIES by Title word(s) (via PSINet) <?>
         5.  Find GOPHER DIRECTORIES by Title word(s) (via U. Nac. Autonoma <?>
         6.  Frequently-Asked Questions (FAQ) about veronica - January 13, 1995
         7.  How to Compose veronica Queries - June 23, 1994
         8.  More veronica: Software, Index-Control Protocol, HTML Pages/
   -->   9.  Search GopherSpace by Title word(s) (via NYSERNet) <?>
        10.  Search GopherSpace by Title word(s) (via PSINet) <?>
        11.  Search GopherSpace by Title word(s) (via U. Nac. Autonoma de MX <?>
             Simplified veronica chooses server - pick a search type:
        13.  Simplified veronica: Find Gopher MENUS only <?>
        14.  Simplified veronica: find ALL gopher types <?>
```

```
          15. how-to-query-veronica
          16. veronica-faq




Press ? for Help, q to Quit, u to go up a menu                    Page: 1/1
```

You can see that I have lots of choices. I select option 9 to perform a search of Gopherspace by a title word. A search screen that prompts me for the words to search for appears. I enter *periodic table*:

```
Internet Gopher Information Client v2.0.16


              Search titles in Gopherspace using veronica


      3.  Find GOPHER DIRECTORIES by Title word(s) (via NYSERNet) <?>
      4.  Find GOPHER DIRECTORIES by Title word(s) (via PSINet) <?>
+-------------Search GopherSpace by Title word(s) (via NYSERNet)--------------+
|                                                                             |
| Words to search for                                                         |
|                                                                             |
|                                                                             |
|              periodic table                                                 |
|                                                                             |
| [Help: ^-]   [Cancel: ^G]                                                   |
+-----------------------------------------------------------------------------+
     13. Simplified veronica: Find Gopher MENUS only <?>
     14. Simplified veronica: find ALL gopher types <?>
     15. how-to-query-veronica
     16. veronica-faq




Press ? for Help, q to Quit, u to go up a menu                    Page: 1/1
```

After a few seconds, the list of periodic tables is shown. I can then type in the number of the option I want to view or move the arrow keys to point to my choice and press return.

```
          Internet Gopher Information Client v2.0.16


          Search GopherSpace by Title word(s) (via NYSERNet): periodic table


   -->  1.   Periodic Table of Elements/
        2.   Periodic Table of the Elements
        3.   Periodic Table
        4.   Periodic Table
        5.   Periodic Table, Facts & Copyright
        6.   Periodic Table
        7.   Periodic Table
        8.   Periodic Table
        9.   Re: Periodic Table of the Elements
       10.   Periodic Table of the Elements
       11.   Re: Periodic Table of the Elements
       12.   Periodic Table
```

```
13. xpt              [volume19]:  xpt      - An X Periodic Table/
14. xpt              [volume20]:  xpt      - An X Periodic Table/
15. [volume19] xpt              :  xpt      - An X Periodic Table/
16. [volume20] xpt              :  xpt      - An X Periodic Table/
17. xview_periodic    : XVIEW Periodic table  - Illustrates objects/
18. Periodic_Table.ps


Press ? for Help, q to Quit, u to go up a menu          Page: 1/12
```

I can now select any of the first 12 sites shown and find the information that I am looking for concerning atomic weights.

5.3 USING JUGHEAD TO SEARCH GOPHERSPACE

Jughead is a tool very similar to Veronica, except for one major difference: Veronica tries to cover all of Gopherspace, while Jughead looks at a confined space in depth. Jughead is not nearly as widespread as Veronica, since Jughead requires the systems administrator at each gopher site to construct a local database for Jughead to use. When Jughead's search window pops up, you can fill it out exactly as you did for the one on Veronica.

If you want to try a Jughead search, point your gopher client to the University of Utah's gopher site *gopher.utah.edu*. In addition, you can get a list of all Jughead servers from this site by selecting the "all known Jughead servers" menu option.

In addition to performing the standard boolean searches that we performed on Veronica, Jughead supports a few special ones:

?all *what*	Returns all matches on search string *what*
?help [command]	Returns help document and any optional matches for the given command
?limit=*n what*	Returns up to *n* items matching the search string *what*

5.4 A FINAL GOPHER USE

The gopher at the University of Wisconsin at Madison has a main-menu option labeled "Phone Books" that contains white pages of people on the Internet. Another gopher site with this type of data is the gopher at Notre Dame, *gopher.nd.edu* which has a menu option of "Non-Notre Dame Information Sources/Phone Books—Other Institutions." This option gives you access to hundreds of white-page directories for schools, companies, and the government.

A good source for college e-mail addresses is *pit-manager.mit.edu* in the directory */pub/usenet/soc.college*, from which they can be FTPed.

5.5 WAIS

WAIS (pronounced ways), which stands for Wide Area Information Server, searches for words in documents. WAIS goes beyond gopher, FTP, and Archie in that it searches for all kinds of information: text, sounds, programs, graphic images, and animation.

5.5.1 How Do I Use WAIS?

There are two ways to use WAIS: through use a local WAIS program on your computer and by telnet to a public WAIS client or through e-mail.

Both methods work fundamentally the same way: a box pops up to request keywords to search for. The following is a listing of Public U.S. WAIS clients listed by state:

State	Hostname	Login as:
CA	*swais.cwis.uci.edu*	swais
MA	*nnsc.nsf.net*	wais
MA	*quake.think.com*	wais
NC	*kudzu.cnidr.org*	wais
NC	*sunsite.unc.edu*	swais

5.5.2 An Example of the Use of WAIS

Let us start by telneting to *sunsite.unc.edu*. Once we log in as swais, we should type vt100 when prompted for the terminal type.

```
nova{sjames}20% telnet sunsite.unc.edu
Trying 152.2.254.81 ...
Connected to sunsite.unc.edu.
Escape character is '^]'.


UNIX(r) System V Release 4.0 (calzone)

**************** Welcome to SunSITE.unc.edu ****************

SunSITE offers several public services via login. These include:

Lynx is broken temporarily. It'll be back shortly.

Use lynx the simple WWW client to access gopher and Web areas
For a simple WAIS client (over 500 databases),  login as swais
For WAIS search of political databases,          login as politics
For WAIS search of LINUX databases,              login as linux

For a FTP session, ftp to sunsite.unc.edu. Then login as anonymous

For more information about SunSITE, send mail to
info@sunsite.unc.edu

login: swais
Last login: Mon Aug 19 11:02:16 from nova.kettering.edu

University of North Carolina Office For Information Technology
in cooperation with Sun Microsystems, Inc.

Materials available via this id are subject to the statements in
DISCLAIMER.readme found in the anonymous ftp area or on the main menu
of the SunSITE.unc.edu gopher

You could be running this code on your own machine.
You'll find it and other WAIS stuff available via anonymous ftp
```

```
from SunSITE.unc.edu in the pub/packages/infosystems/wais
directory.

These databases are also available via gopher.
Just point your gopher client to sunsite.unc.edu 70
and enjoy using these databases from your gopher interface.

you're probably a vt100 or should be
TERM = (unknown) vt100
```

We will now be presented with a screen listing the various databases. We need to select our sources, which we do by using the arrow keys. We press the space bar to select a source, and an asterisk appears next to the source to indicate that we have selected it. Do not worry about the "cost" field; all the sources are free! You can select as many sources as you wish before searching. If you are going to start a new search, you should press the equals (=) key to deselect all of your old sources if you do not intend to search all of them.

```
SWAIS                     Source Selection          Sources: 82
   #            Server                 Source          Cost
 001:  [      sunsite.unc.edu]  alt-sys-sun            Free
 002:  [                     ]  American-Music-Resource  Free
 003:  [                     ]  avi_files              Free
 004:  [            calypso]  bush-speeches            Free
 005:  [                     ]  carter-oh              Free
 006:  [                     ]  clinton-speeches       Free
 007:  [                     ]  clinton-speechess      Free
 008:  [      sunsite.unc.edu]  Community-IdeaNet       Free
 009:  [                     ]  Davis-eis-cds          Free
 010:  [                     ]  Davis-eiscds           Free
 011:  [                     ]  Davis-music-eam        Free
 012:  [                     ]  Davis-music-jazz       Free
 013:  [                     ]  Davis-music-rbr        Free
 014:  [                     ]  Davis-music-vids       Free
 015:  [calypso-2.oit.unc.ed]  Dr-Fun                 Free
 016:  [                     ]  eisenhower-oh          Free
 017:  [      sunSITE.unc.edu]  eric-digests           Free
 018:  [      sunsite.unc.edu]  Fascism                Free

Keywords:

<space>  selects, w for keywords, arrows move, <return> searches,
q quits, or ?
```

Once you have selected your sources, press return to go to the "Keywords" line. Enter all the keywords you want to match. Say that we want to search for information on President Clinton's health care reforms. We could search for Clinton health reform. After we enter the keywords, we press the return key to start the search.

```
SWAIS                     Source Selection          Sources: 82
   #            Server                 Source          Cost
 019:  [         bittyblue]  foo                      Free
 020:  [                   ]  ford-finding-aids        Free
 021:  [calypso-2.oit.unc.ed]  freeburma              Free
 022:  [            calypso]  govnii                   Free
 023:  [            calypso]  govnpr                   Free
```

```
024: * [            calypso]   govradio                    Free
025: * [ calypso.oit.unc.edu]   Health-Security-Act         Free
026: * [          president]   index                       Free
027:   [            calypso]   INFO                        Free
028:   [    sunsite.unc.edu]   Jainist-texts               Free
029     calypso-2.oit.unc.ed]   java                        Free
030:   [                   ]   johnson-oh                  Free
031:   [            calypso]   lawrence-obrien-interview   Free
032:   [    sunsite.unc.edu]   linux-addresses             Free
033                        ]   linux-faq                   Free
034:   [            calypso]   linux-gcc-faq               Free
035:   [            calypso]   linux-net-faq               Free
036:   [                   ]   linux-software-map          Free
```

Keywords: **Clinton health reform**

Once the search is done, you can perform another search or you can examine what was returned by moving to the appropriate line and pressing the return key. WAIS will then contact the source of the document and pull up a copy of the document. If you like what you see and want to keep a copy of it, press either *s* for save or *m* for mail. As usual, you can use *q* to stop viewing a document. Be careful, though, because *q* also quits the WAIS program.

5.6 PERFORMING A WAIS SEARCH VIA E-MAIL

Performing a WAIS search via e-mail is fairly simple. Send a message to *wais-mail@quake.think.com* such that the body of the message is the command *search sourcename keywords*. *Sourcename* is the database name(s) to search and keywords are what you want to search for. When you get your results back, you can retrieve the documents by sending another e-mail message to the server with a message body of *retrieve DocID*. The *DocID* will be supplied along with your WAIS results.

PRACTICE!

Use the WAIS e-mail service to look up a topic that will have several responses. Try sending the following e-mail message:

```
To: waismail@quake.think.com
Subject:
Message:   search clinton-speeches education
```

Since the *clinton-speeches* database has President Clinton's speeches contained within, there should be a few items on education in the database.

5.7 THE FUTURE OF WAIS

As you may have noticed, this section on WAIS was very short. The reason for its brevity is that the future of WAIS is limited. There are several publicly available search engines on the World Wide Web that do as good a job as WAIS does without having to specify any databases. We will spend time examining these types of searches later. As search systems become more integrated into packages, WAIS may indeed become an archaic system.

SUMMARY

This chapter examined the Internet entities gopher and WAIS. Both of these resources provide a menu-based approach to retrieving information from the Internet. The primary difference between the two resources lies in the fact that WAIS requires that the user select databases from which a search is executed, while Gopher only requires that the user enters keywords, after which gopherspace is examined for matching information. The future of both of these items is in doubt due to the exponential growth of Web browsers and the publicly available search engines that can be accessed by them.

KEY TERMS

Client	Gopherspace	Server
Document	Item	Veronica
Gopher	Jughead	WAIS

Problems

1. Find out if your school has a gopher site. Use your gopher software to access it.
2. Point your gopher client at *gopher.house.gov* and find out who your state representatives are. Print out the information on one of your representatives. (*Note:* if you do not have a gopher client, telnet to one of the publicly available ones.)
3. Use Veronica to find out where the periodic tables are stored on the Web. Then locate and print out the information related to the element molybdenum.
4. Use WAIS to look up what President Bush had to say about reform. Try using "bush speeches" as your data source and "reform" as your keyword.

6

The World Wide Web and HTML

SCIENCE/ENGINEERING SPOTLIGHT: ROBOTICS

We often think of robots as mobile machines equipped with artificial intelligence. Science-fiction books and movies certainly have contributed to this: R2D2 and C3PO from Star Wars embody this vision. Today, robots really are best suited for the manufacturing process. Robots can help in assembly operations, inspection operations, and in packaging/palettizing. In addition, many robots today have special end effectors that allow them to perform welding, material removal, painting, and adhesive application.

OBJECTIVES

After reading this chapter, you should be able to:

- Explain what a browser, a home page, and a URL are
- Create your own web page
- Describe what an add-in is and how to use one

This chapter will examine what is considered the state of the art with respect to the Internet today: the World Wide Web. A discussion of web browsers and their capabilities are examined. The chapter then provides information on creating HTML Web pages. The chapter concludes with a look at some of the newer extensions to the Web. Let us start by looking at what WWW is all about.

6.1   WWW: THE WORLD WIDE WEB

All the other services that we have viewed up to this point have been primarily text based in nature. The Web, although it has a textual side, was designed to be primarily graphical in nature. In fact, Web *browsers* are a point-and-click approach to accessing the Internet.

WWW has combined text, graphics, audio, and even animation into a multimedia event. Each page that you view with your Web browser is typically linked to other pages around the Internet, and you can directly move from location to location with the click of a mouse. Should a particular page have an audio file, your computer can retrieve and play that sound if your computer is equipped with audio capabilities. You do not have to look at plain graphic screens only; your computer can download moving images and play them for you as well.

The best feature of the Web is probably the fact that the same interface is used to move around the Internet; to seamlessly access Internet services such as FTP, Gopher, and UseNet News; and to supply powerful search engines that are starting to replace WAIS.

6.1.1   WWW-Related Terms

The following is list of terms that deal with the World Wide Web with which you should familiarize yourself before moving on:

Browser: A browser is the program that you use to access the hypertext documents on the Web. Browsers are also responsible for showing you animations and graphics and playing sounds as long as your computer is equipped to do so. Browsers come in two types: text and graphic.

Text browsers show you only the text on each of the pages; however, you can move between pages by pressing the cursor keys. There are two main text browsers available: *www* and *lynx*.

Graphic browsers are the full blown program that you usually see when someone says they're "surfing the 'Net." There are several graphic browsers used today: *Mosaic*, Microsoft's *Internet Explorer*, and *Netscape*.

Within any browser, you have the ability to configure other programs that can handle a specific document type. For example, I can set up my PC to run a sound player when the browser encounters any .au file. In this respect, you can "upgrade" your computer to take advantage of whatever aspects of the Web you feel are important.

Cookies: Little pieces of information stored on your local computer about the last interaction you made with a specific Web site. The next time that you access that same Web site, it will read the cookie from your local machine.

HTTP: Hypertext Transport Protocol is the protocol that allows the hypertext pages on the Web to be quickly retrieved.

Home Pages: Most WWW users can create their own home page, which may have information on the user or may serve as a repository for the user's favorite Web sites. Home pages, as well as any other Web pages, must be built with HTML. There are many programs available that can help a user quickly create HTML pages. The second half of this chapter will assist you in creating HTML pages.

HTML: HTML is the special formatting used to create a page on the Web. HTML stands for Hypertext Markup Language and is a set of basic commands that are placed around objects in a document with instructions about how an object is to be displayed, where the object is to be located, how to link to another page, and so on.

Hypertext: Hypertext is text that contains a link to an other object. You know when a particular text is hypertext because it is a different color than normal text. (On some browsers, it may be underlined.) Documents form links with more than just text are called *hypermedia*.

Links: Links are references to other documents on the Web.

URL: URL stands for Uniform Resource Locator which is a Web standard on how to locate an item that is to be retrieved. There are two types of URLs: *absolute,* which require the full computer name, path name and item name; and *relative,* which assumes that the previous computer and directory names are to be used. A typical URL might look like *http://defiant.kettering.edu/~sjames*.

As you might have guessed, the first part of the URL is the *protocol service* to use. After the colon and the two slashes come the *computer name* and *path name*. The very end of the URL contains the item name. Our example thus tells the browser to retrieve the item *sjames* from the computer *defiant.kettering.edu* using the *http* protocol.

Other protocols that can be used in a browser include:

Service	Use
archie	starts an Archie session
finger	starts up the finger program
ftp	starts an FTP session
gopher	starts a gopher session
mailto	starts an e-mail program
news	starts a UseNet News session
telnet	starts a TELNET session
wais	accesses a WAIS server
whois	accesses a whois server

Web Server: A Web server is a computer that contains home pages that are to be supplied to browsers for people that wish to view them.

6.1.2 A Sample Web Browser

Notice that when compared to plain text, browsers, graphical Web browsers add much more meaning to information they retrieve.

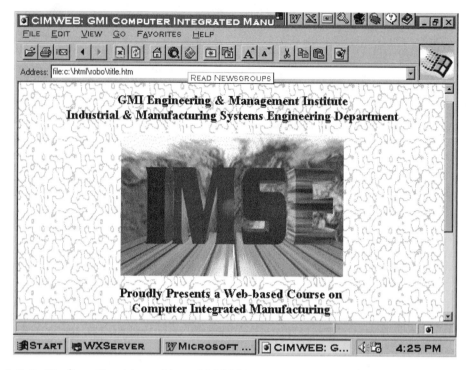

6.1.3 Finding Out More About WWW

If you want to find out more about the Web and what can be done with it, here are a few places to start:

UseNet Newsgroups

comp.infosystems.www.misc	how to do most WWW related tasks
comp.infosystems.www.providers	how to set up a WWW server
comp.infosystems.www.users	how to use and set up client software

Mailing Lists

You can send e-mail to *listserv@info.cern.ch* with *subscribe <list> yourrealname* as the body of the message. The list needs to be one of the following:

www-announce	discusses current-state and new software
www-html	talks about the HTML language
www-talk	technical discussions of WWW software design

WWW Sites

http://info.cern.ch/hypertext/WWW/TheProject.html	World Wide Web Initiative
http://www.ncsa.uiuc.edu/demoweb/demo.html	NCSA Mosaic Demo Document
http://www.internic.net	InterNIC
http://www.eit.com/web/www.guide	Entering the WWW: A Guide to Cyberspace

6.1.4 A Few Web Sites to Start with

If you are new on the Web and want a few interesting sites with wich to play around, you might want to check out these sites:

http://defiant.kettering.edu	The coolest professors hang out here
http://galaxy.einet.net/galaxy.html	EINet Galaxy Search Engine
http://hypatia.gsfc.nasa.gov/NASA_homepage.html	NASA
http://info.er.usgs.gov	U.S. Geological Survey
http://lcweb.loc.gov/homepage/lchp.html	Library of Congress
http://med-www.Stanford.EDU/MedCenter/welcome.html	Stanford University Medical Center
http://metaverse.com	Adam Curry's site
http://mistral.enst.fr/louvre	The Louvre online
http://netvet.wustl.edu/e-zoo.htm	Electronic Zoo
http://pubweb.parc.xerox.com/map	Xerox PARC Map Viewer
http://shop.internic.net	Internet Shopping Netowrk
http://tns-www.lcs.mit.edu/tns-www.home.html	MIT Cutting Edge
http://voyager.paramount.com	Star Trek: Voyager site
http://wings.buffalo.edu/world/	Virtual Tourist
http://www.cl.cam.ac.uk/coffee/coffee.html	The Trojan Room Coffee Machine
http://www.commerce.net	CommerceNet
http://www.fedworld.gov	FedWorld
http://www.hotwired.com	HotWired Magazine
http://www.internet.nic/directories.html	Infoworld's Web page
http://www.internic.net	InterNIC Home Page
http://www.microsoft.com	Microsoft Web page
http://www.msstate.edu/Movies	Cardiff's Movie Database
http://www.os.dhhs.gov	U.S. Deptartment of Health and Human Services
http://www.scotborders.co.uk:80/dryburgh/dryburghmap.html	An area map
http://www.timeinc.com/pathfinder/Welcome.html	Time/Warner's Pathfinder
http://www.whitehouse.gov	The White House
http://www.worldbank.org	The World Bank

6.1.5 Search Sites

Where can you go if you are looking for something on the web, but do not know where it is located or what it is called? You need to use a *search engine*. The following is a list of popular sites:

Alta Vista	*http://www.altavista.digital.com*
ArchiePlex	*http://pubweb.nexor.co.uk/public/archie/archieplex/doc/form.html*
EINET	*http://www.einet.net/www/www.html*
Excite	*http://www.excite.com*
Infoseek	*http://www.infoseek.com*
Lycos	*http://lycos.cs.cmu.edu*
WebCrawler	*http://webcrawler.cs.washington.edu/WebCrawler/WebQuery.html*
Whole Internet Catalog	*http://www.gnn.com/wic/newrescat.toc.html*
World Wide Web Word	*http://www.cs.colorado.edu/home/mcbryan/wwww.html*
Yahoo	*http://www.yahoo.com*

PROFESSIONAL SUCCESS:
TIPS ON USING SEARCH ENGINES

Search engines such as those previously listed are constantly getting more effective and efficient in terms of the information that they return to you. You still need to do some intelligent searching when you work with them, however.

Let's say that I want to find Visual Basic graphics programs. Typing these words into the search box on most of the search engines will bring back thousands of potential pages, most of which will not relate to what I am looking for. I can make the search more limited by looking for the words "Visual Basic" graphic. By wrapping quotes around words that have spaces in them, you can force most search engines to use the quoted material as a single search word rather than as multiple words. In addition, many search engines allow you to search for all pages containing a particular subject (such as "Visual Basic") and then do a subsearch for an additional topic within those pages (such as "graphic").

Another tip related to searching is that you should consult several different search engines for the same material. You will be very surprised to see the different pages that each engine pulls up. Some pages that are important to you may appear on only one of the search engines that you try.

Finally, favor search engines that provide feedback on how well each page fits your search criteria. Engines like Excite and Infoseek, for example, provide a percentage of how well a Web page matches your criteria. From personal experience, I have found that most pages rated under 65% usually do not pertain to what I am looking for. You should adopt a percentage threshold below which you ignore results after you have gained some experience in searching. This procedure will help to save your time and to maximize the usefulness of information returned to you from a search engine.

APPLICATION:
LOCATING INFORMATION ON THE INTERNET

This application will take a closer look at some of the information that is contained on the Internet. I will be using the Excite search engine to find this information. Search engines allow you to look up any subject in which you are interested and then return Web sites that contain information pertaining (sometimes!) to what you are looking for.

I begin by pointing my browser to *http://www.excite.com,* which brings up the following page:

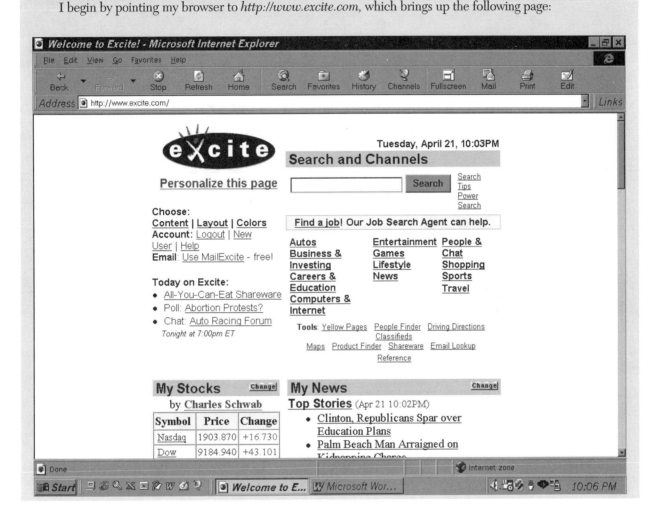

Notice that I can type a topic in the "Search" box and then press the "Search" button. Most search engines work in this fashion. In addition to being able to look up topical information, I can create maps, look up business phone numbers, and try to locate people all through this single resource.

In the first example, I want to create a map showing me where Kettering University is. I begin by clicking on the Maps tool, which is located in the middle of the right-hand side of the Web page. I am then presented with the next Web page, which allows me to quickly map U.S. cities or states. I am going to map a U.S. address in Michigan, for which the selection is located in the middle of the right-hand side of the Web page again:

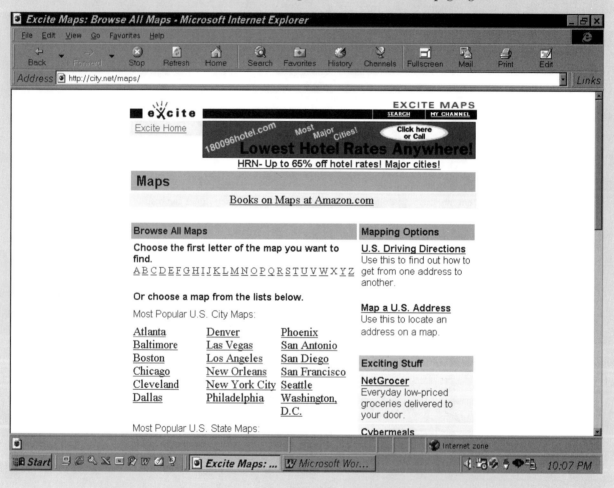

In the next Web page, I actually enter the address of the location that I wish to map. You can see that I have entered Kettering University's address. Now I need only click on the "Map It" button to create the map.

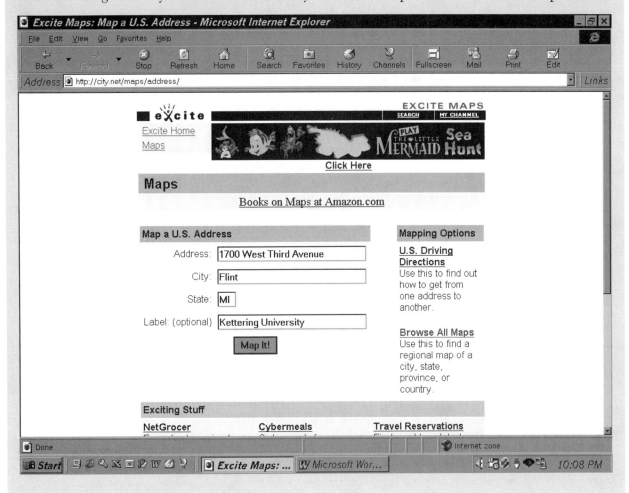

The next Web page shows you the results. Also notice that I have been provided with navigation tools under the map that allow me to zoom in or out and to move around in the map.

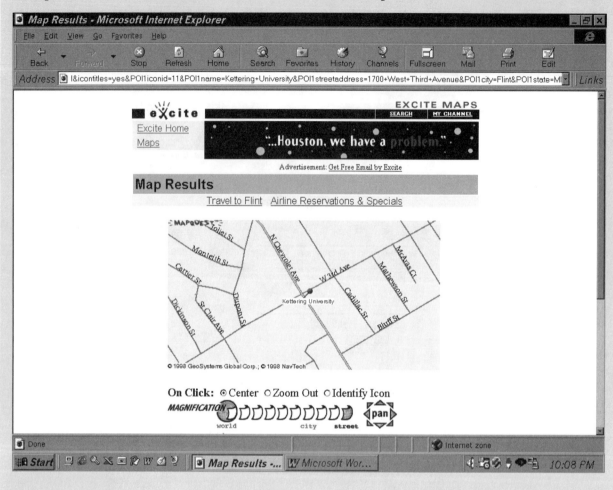

My next example shows how to locate information on a particular topic through the use of a search engine. Let us say that I want to find out more information about stereolithography. If you do not know what Stereolithography is, the Internet is an ideal way to get an introduction to this exciting rapid prototyping technology.

All that I need to do is return to the main Excite search page, enter my query, and press the "Search" button:

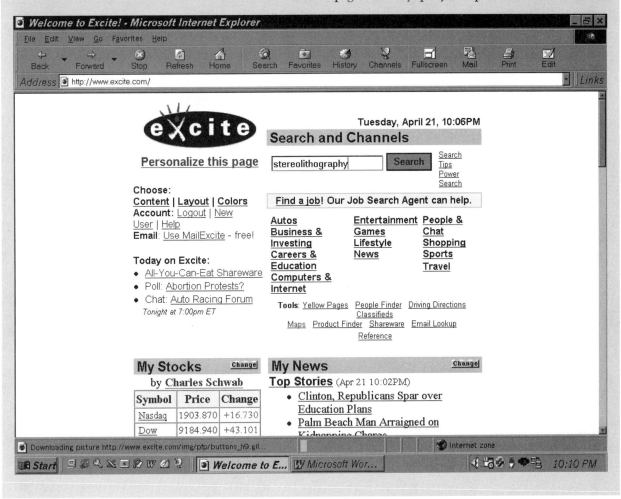

You can see on the next Web page a portion of the list of Web sites that have information pertaining to stereolithography. Many of the Web sites shown have some relevance to what I am searching for. There are some that do not, though, so this search method is by no means foolproof for returning "good" information.

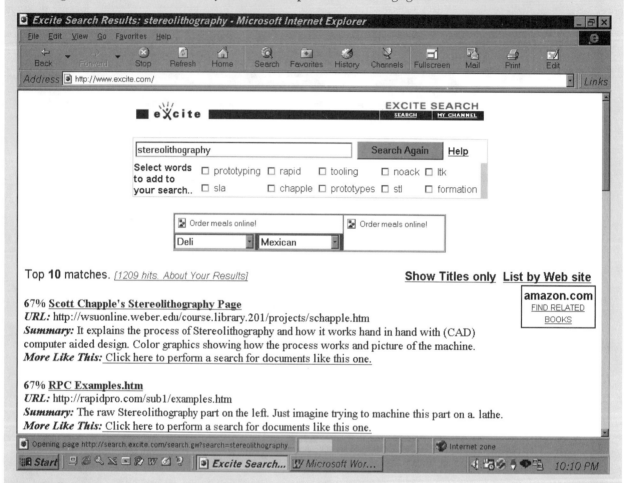

Following just about any of the links will take you to Web sites that both describe what the stereolithography process is and includes some sample parts that were created by using the process.

PRACTICE!

This practice set is concerned with using a Web browser.

1. Try using your browser to view the home page of my department, which is located at the URL *http://defiant.kettering.edu*. If you are successful, you should see a page similar to the one previously shown in the sample Web browser example.

2. Point your Web browser to the URL *http://www.yahoo.com*. Enter *Clinton health reform* in the search box. Notice how much easier this type of search is in comparison to Veronica or WAIS.

6.2 CREATING WEB PAGES WITH HTML

HTML pages can be created in several different ways. There are graphical web-creation tools that provide users with tool palettes from which the different HTML elements may be selected. HTML pages can also be created with a text editor.

While a text editor may be more time consuming to work with, it is important to note that all HTML pages are actually text based. This section will provide an introduction to creating HTML pages from a completely text-based perspective.

Once you have created an HTML page, you must put the page on a Web server so that other users on the Internet can see your page. It is beyond the scope of this module to explain to you where to put the page, how to get the page on the Web server, and so forth. Even the name of the initial HTML page may have to be something specific, such as Welcome.html or Home.html, depending on your local computer system. Therefore, it is important that you obtain some help in answering the issues that are specific to your computer resources.

You should bear in mind that none of these factors will limit you in creating HTML pages. You can still create a page on any computer that has a browser. After the page is created, point the browser at the page to view it.

6.2.1 The Basic HTML Page

All HTML pages have the following skeleton form:

```
<HTML>
<BODY>
</BODY>
</HTML>
```

HTML uses what are known as *tags*. You put tags around items that are to appear in your HTML page. The tag acts as a display attribute for a given item. For example, if I want to underline some text on an HTML page, I need to turn on the underlining feature, type the text that I want to underline, and then turn off the underlining feature. This turning-on-and-turning-off process is the use of a tag.

From the given skeleton form, you can see that all HTML pages must start with the <HTML> tag. Anything that appears inside of the < > marks is part of the HTML language and will not literally be shown on the HTML page. Just as all pages start with <HTML>, they must end with </HTML>. Most tags use a / character to indicate that some attribute is to be turned off.

The <BODY> and </BODY> tags are where we will place the meat of our HTML work.

Let us now put together a more complex example, in which I am going to add some information to be displayed on my HTML page.

```
<HTML>
<! *********************************************>
<! *                Example.html              *>
<! *********************************************>
<! *            Created by: Scott D. James      *>
<! *                  On: June 11, 1996        *>
<! *********************************************>
<! * Purpose: To show a simple HTML page.      *>
<! *********************************************>
<TITLE>Scott's First Page</TITLE>
<BODY>
<H1>Hello to the Internet from Scott!</H1>
```

```
<P>
I'm glad you stopped by...
<BR>
Created 06/11/96 by Scott D. James
</BODY>
</HTML>
```

Notice that both the `<HTML>` and `<BODY>` tags appear, in addition to a host of new tags. The first new tag starts with `<!`. This tag indicates that I want to put some comments into the HTML source. These comments will not be shown on the HTML page, but are useful for documenting how or why I did something. Anything between the `<!   >` is the comment.

The next tag is the `<TITLE>` tag. This tag indicates that what follows it will appear in the title of the browser's window. If you examine the actual browser screen that follows, you will notice the title says "Scott's First Page." An accompanying `</TITLE>` must be used to end the title-bar text.

Following the `<TITLE>` section is the `<BODY>` section, which usually contains the main information that is to be displayed on the HTML page. I surrounded some of the text with the `<H1>` and `</H1>` tags. These tags are used to indicate that I want the text to be displayed as a bold heading.

The `<P>` tag is simply a paragraph marker, which inserts a blank line between the header and the regular text in this case. Please realize that return keystrokes placed in the HTML source file are for our purposes only; HTML ignores those returns and will only process the HTML tags that are placed in the source.

The next line is a bit of text that I want to appear on the page. I used the `<BR>` tag to separate the two regular text lines on the HTML page, in other words, `<BR>` acts as a return command. You can think of BR as a line break. It is how we get returns to show up on our pages.

Finally, I use the `</BODY>` and `</HTML>` tags to end the body section and HTML section. Here is how the page appears in a browser:

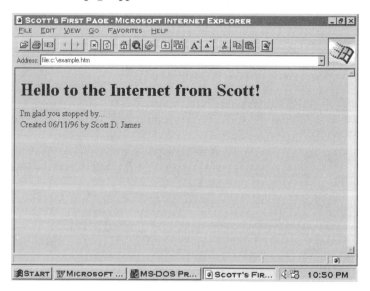

The HTML page has a pretty nice appearance for the little bit of work that it took to create it. You should realize by now that tags surround text and act as attributes of how that text is to be displayed. Tags can be placed inside of other tags, and HTML can even be written as a long line if we so desire. For example,

```
<HTML><TITLE>Hi There!</TITLE><BODY>Isn't this fun?</BODY></HTML>
```

is a perfectly valid command.

You should try to create a simple HTML page and view it with a browser before moving on. Any text editor, such as MS-DOS' edit or UNIX VI, will work fine. The most common mistake that you will encounter is that you might forget to close " " or < >. If you do not close these items, the browser you are using will do its best to try to display the HTML page, but things do not look the way they should, check to ensure that these items have been properly closed.

PRACTICE!

> Let us create an HTML page that has the following information on it: the author's name and the slogan "I love HTML!" The slogan appear very large in size. Let us also put the title "HMTL Is Easy" on the title bar.
>
> You should type in the following code, save it, and then view it with your browser.
>
> ```
> <HTML>
> <TITLE>HTML Is Easy</TITLE>
> <BODY>
> This page was written by (* your name here *)<BR>
> <P>
> <H1>I Love HTML!</H1>
> </BODY>
> </HTML>
> ```

6.2.2 Text-formatting Tags

It is now time to examine other ways to change the appearance of text on Web pages. The list that follows is not exhaustive, but it still embodies the tags that are most commonly used. Since HTML is an expanding universe, you need to check the current standard to find out which other extensions are available.

Tag	Meaning
<P>	Paragraph mark—used to divide text sections
 	Line break—acts like a return on the HMTL page
<Hn> </Hn>	Heading tags—n can range from 1 to 6
<B> </B>	Bold text
<I> </I>	Italics text
<U> </U>	Underlined text
<BLOCKQUOTE> </BLOCKQUOTE>	Double-indented text
<NOBR> </NOBR>	No line breaks in text
<CENTER> </CENTER>	Center
<CODE> </CODE>	Computer code
<PRE> </PRE>	Keeps tabs and breaks as they appear in the editor (text is formatted)

Let us look at some of these tags through the browser's eye:

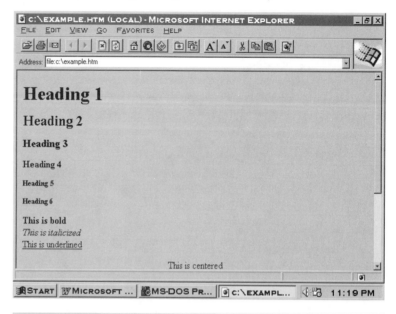

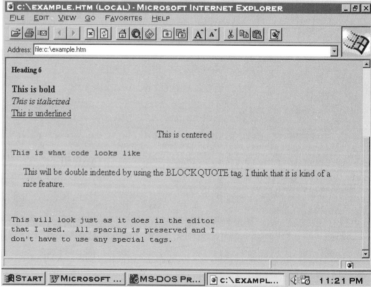

Here is the accompanying HTML code that produced this page:

```
<HTML>
<BODY>
<H1>Heading 1</H1> <H2>Heading 2</H2>
<H3>Heading 3</H3> <H4>Heading 4</H4>
<H5>Heading 5</H5> <H6>Heading 6</H6> <P>
<B>This is bold</B><BR>
<I>This is italicized</I><BR>
<U>This is underlined</U><BR><BR>
<CENTER>This is centered</CENTER>
<P>
<CODE>This is what code looks like<CODE><BR>
```

```
<BLOCKQUOTE>This will be double indented by using the
BLOCKQUOTE tag. I think that it is kind of a nice feature.
</BLOCKQUOTE><BR>
<PRE>
This will look just as it does in the editor
that I used.  All spacing is preserved and I
don't have to use any special tags.
</PRE>
</BODY>
</HTML>
```

6.2.3 Other Text Gadgets

One task that we often need to perform in our HTML pages is that of creating lists. There are two types of lists that we can create: unordered (or bulleted) and ordered (or numbered). Unordered lists have the skeleton frame of:

```
<UL>
[<UL TYPE = [circle|disk|square]>]
<LI>First choice
<LI>Second choice
<LI>nth choice
</UL>
```

Unordered lists use a circle as the default list-item divider. If you want, you can change the circle to a disk or square by supplying the UL TYPE tag.

The code for ordered lists looks very similar to that for unordered lists except that for ordered lists, we use OL instead of UL. The OL TYPE can be one of:

a : Lowercase letters

A : Uppercase letters

i : Lowercase roman numbers

I : Uppercase roman numbers

1 : Arabic numbers (This is the default.)

Here is how we might create a nested list (a list within a list) using several of the list elements:

```
<HTML>
<BODY>
<UL>
<LI>Things I like about HTML:
<OL>
<LI>It's fun
<LI>It's easy
<LI>It's fast
</OL>
<LI>Things I like about the Internet:
<OL>
<OL TYPE=i>
<LI>It's easy to use
<LI>My friends are using it
<LI>Anyone can contact me 24 hours a day
<LI>It's a lot of fun
</OL>
</UL>
</BODY>
</HTML>
```

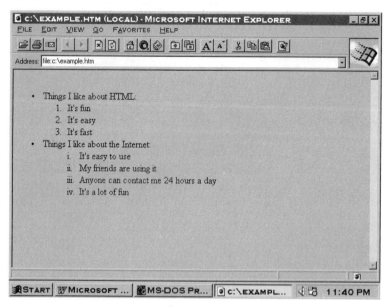

Sometimes, you may want to break up a long page with some lines. The <HR> Horizontal rule tag accomplishes this task. Its attributes are:

```
<HR>
<HR SIZE=n>                   The line will be n points high
<HR NOSHADE>                  Plain line
<HR WIDTH=[n|p%]>             The line will be n pixels long or p% of the page
```

Here is an example of the four types of horizontal rule as they appear in the browser:

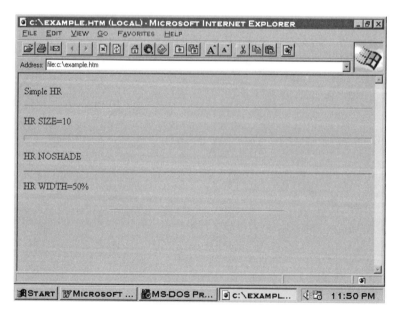

6.2.4 Working with Images

Text is only one facet of what can be included on HTML pages. The other item that we frequently see is graphics. If you have any GIF-formatted images that you wish to display in your HTML page, use the IMG SRC tag. The format is:

```
<IMG SRC="URL to image"
[ALIGN="TOP|BOTTOM|MIDDLE|LEFT|RIGHT|TEXTTOP|ABSMIDDLE|BASELINE"]
[ALT="text"] [BORDER=n] [VSPACE=n] [HSPACE=n]>
```

where

- "URL to image" is the path to the graphics file and the name of the graphics file.
- ALIGN refers to the alignment of the image.
- ALT refers to text that is to be displayed in place of the image to text-based browsers.
- BORDER refers to the point width (n) of the border that surrounds the image.
- VSPACE offsets the image n points from the left/right margin of the page.
- HSPACE offsets the image n points from the upper/lower margin of the page.

Let us examine HTML code for the incorporation of graphics with the following HTML page:

```
<HTML>
<BODY>
<! Just stick the image in>
<IMG SRC="\HTML\IMSE.GIF">
<P>
<! Let's put the image in a second time and flow the text around it>
<! Also add in the ALT tag so that text based viewers can see some-
thing>
<IMG SRC="\HTML\IMSE.GIF" ALT="IMSE logo image" ALIGN="LEFT" HSPACE=10>
This text should appear<BR>
next to the image on the<BR>
right hand side of the page<BR>
<P>
</BODY>
</HTML>
```

Here is the resulting browser page (note that the full second image is on the page—I just did not scroll down far enough to show it):

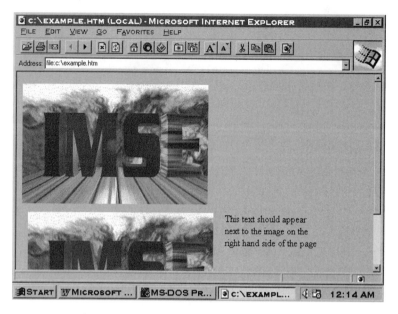

6.2.5 Creating Links

Links are the last item that we need to examine to have a well-rounded view of HTML. The magic behind the Web is the ability to "leap" from page to page. This leaping is what is known as linking. Any displayable entity on an HTML page can become a link. The format for a link is:

```
<A HREF="URL to link to">Item-to-show-up-as-the-link</A>
```

The A comes from Anchor which means that a particular piece of text or image is linked ("anchored") to another page. If you make text into a link, it will show up in a different color from other text. If you make an image a link, the border around the image will be a different color. Let us create two pages and then link the pages to each other. Page 1 HTML Code:

```
<HTML>
<BODY>
<CENTER><H2>Welcome to Page 1!</H2></CENTER>
<A HREF="\page2.htm"><IMG SRC="\HTML\IMSE.GIF" BORDER=7></A>
<CENTER>Click the image or <A HREF="\page2.htm">here</A> to go
to Page 2.
</CENTER>
</BODY>
</HTML>
```

Page 2 HTML Code:

```
<HTML>
<BODY>
<H2>Welcome to page 2!</H2>
Here's the way to <A HREF="\page1.htm">Page 1</A>.
</BODY>
</HTML>
```

Here is what Page 1 looks like in the browser:

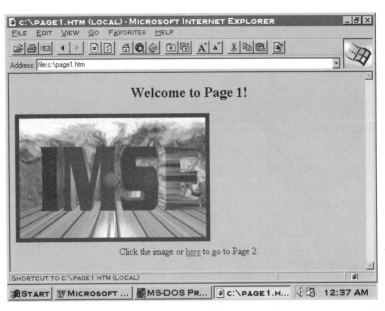

Both the image and the word "here" are links to another HTML page. If I click in either spot, I get to the second page:

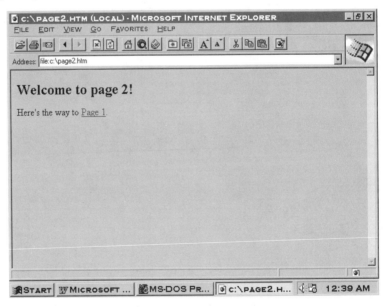

As you can see, Page 2 provides a text link to go back to Page 1.

Many times, the links that we make are not to our own local machine. This situation does not present a problem as long as we identify the remote machine in our URL. For example, I could make a link to a page on my remote machine *defiant*. This is what the link might look like:

```
<A HREF="http://defiant.kettering.edu">To IMSE Homepage</A>
```

By carefully specifying a remote computer's name and the service that you wish to use, you can significantly enhance HTML pages that you are designing. Here are some other examples:

```
<A HREF="telnet://nova.kettering.edu">Click here to telnet to nova</A>
<A HREF="mailto://sjames@nova.kettering.edu">Mail sjames</A>
<A HREF="ftp://oak.oakland.edu">FTP to Oakland University</A>
```

APPLICATION:
HTML PUBLISHING

The preceding section shows how to create HTML pages using a text editor. While it is important to examine HTML code to understand how HTML pages actually work, very few people still produce HTML pages by hand. There are a number of graphical editors that produce entire Web sites through the use of a mouse. Sausage Software's Hot Dog Professional and Microsoft's FrontPage are a couple of examples. In fact, it has become so easy to create HTML pages and Web sites that most common applications will allow you to do so from within the application itself. The purpose of the next example is to examine these concepts.

Say that I have created a document in Microsoft Word and would like to convert it into a Web page. Here is the original document:

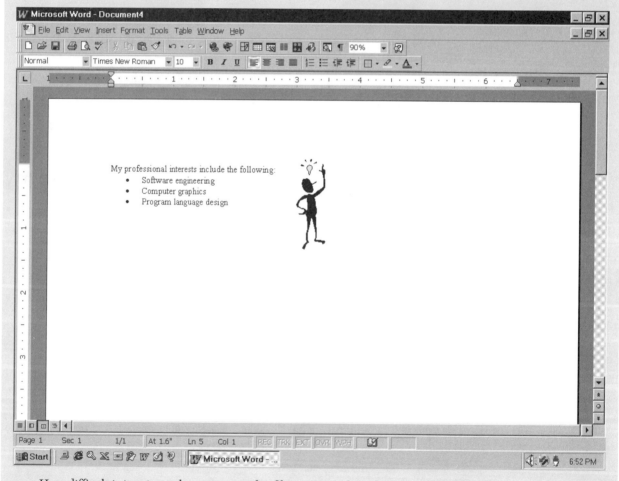

How difficult is it going to be to convert this file to HTML? Under Microsoft Office 97's version of Word, all I need to do is select "Save As HTML" from the file menu and provide a name for the file. So, I do so, calling the file *C:\proint.htm*. Let us take a look at its HTML coding:

```
<HTML>
<HEAD>
<META HTTP-EQUIV="Content-Type" CONTENT="text/html; charset=windows-1252">
<META NAME="Generator" CONTENT="Microsoft Word 97">
<TITLE>My professional interests include the following:</TITLE>
</HEAD>
<BODY>

<P><IMG SRC="Image1.gif" WIDTH=59 HEIGHT=180>My professional interests include the
following:</P>


<UL>
<LI>Software engineering</LI>
<LI>Computer graphics</LI>
<LI>Programming language design</LI></UL>

</BODY>
</HTML>
```

There are some tags in there that I haven't talked about with regard to HTML code, but for the most part, it looks familiar. How does it look as viewed through a browser, though? Let us take a look:

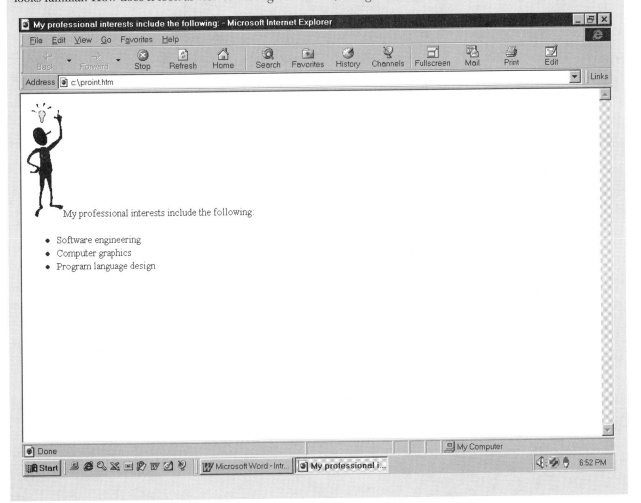

It is not too shabby, considering that I did not, do any work in HTML. Almost all of the large software companies have added this ability to their applications. It empowers the average user to create Web pages.

For the next example, let us look at how Microsoft FrontPage creates an entire Web site. After starting Microsoft FrontPage 98 and telling the program that I want to create a new Web page, I am presented with the following options:

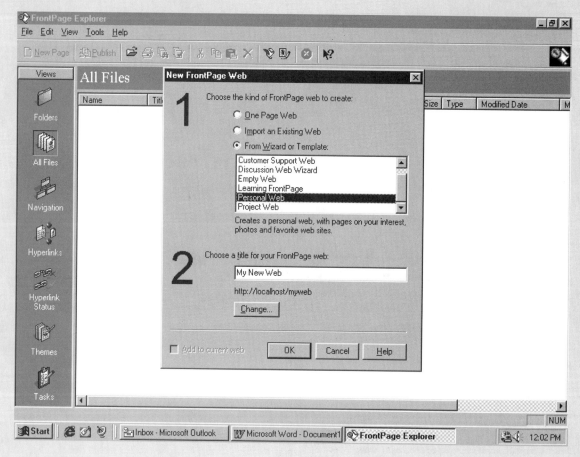

I am going to select a Personal Web page using the Wizard. After clicking on the OK button, a basic Web site is built, containing the following pages:

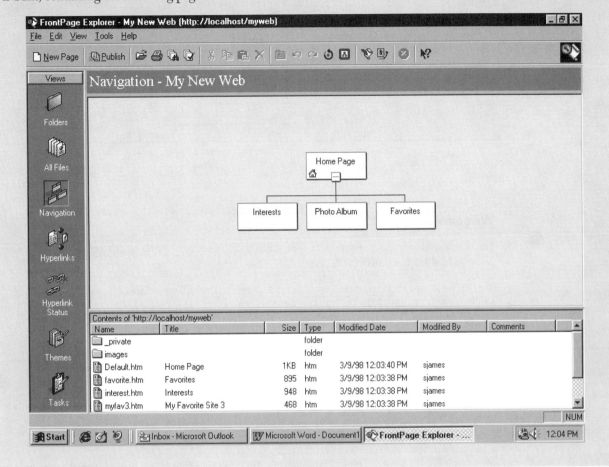

I can now look at the pages and modify them as I see fit, all within the FrontPage program. Let us take a look at what is in the home page by double clicking on it.

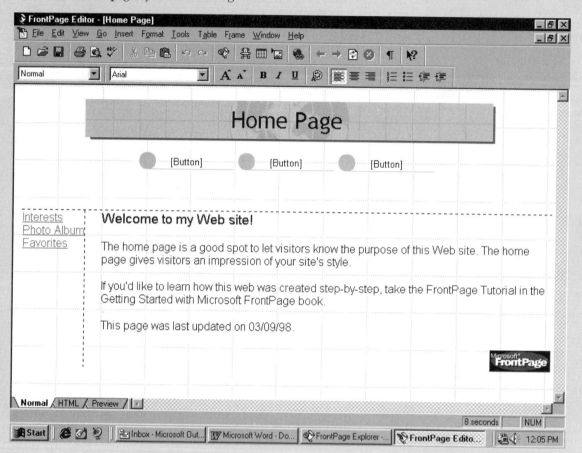

It is not the most exciting page I have created, but it is functional. Notice that there are hyperlinks on the left side of the page that allow me to navigate to the other pages of the series built by FrontPage.

I want to make the page more interesting, so I go back to the FrontPage Explorer and select a different theme. Notice that there are lots of choices available to fit just about any style. I pick the blueprint theme and apply it:

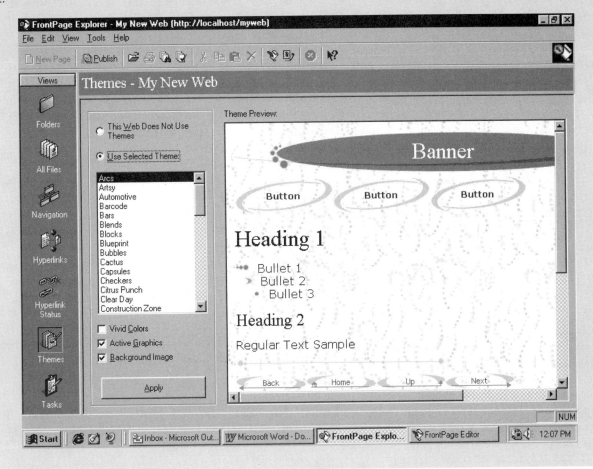

Now we will take a look at that same home page again with the new theme applied to it:

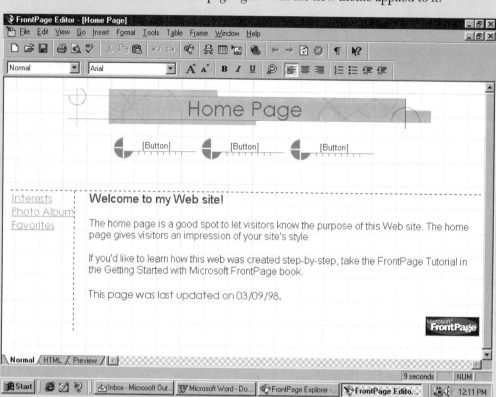

The modifications have made the page look much better. I still have much work to do to finish the Web site, but notice that it took about five mouse clicks to create four pages that are linked together and have a consistent look and feel. Building Web sites and Web pages has become so trivial that anyone can do it with the proper software packages. However, there are still times when it is necessary to adjust the HTML code manually, which is why this chapter still discusses that particular language.

6.3 BROWSER ADD-INS

In addition to all of the power that today's Internet browsers have, there are still enhancements that each user can make to personalize his or her own browser. An add-in is a separate piece of software that is loaded onto the computer on which the browser is located. The installation program of the add-in informs the browser that a new add-in is available. Whenever the browser comes across Web page content that can be processed by the add-in, that particular add-in is started up.

There are many different classes of add-ins available. There are add-in packages that permit actual audio and video information to be sent over the Internet. This particular type of technology is called streaming media. Chapter 7 will look at a couple of examples of this type of add-in.

Another add-in type is the certificate add-in. Many different software vendors offer certificate programs that can be added to a browser. The purpose of the certificate is to verify the authenticity of Web page content such as executable programs. This feature can help Internet users avoid getting bad copies of software that may be infected with viruses and so forth.

Along the same lines as certificate add-ins, there are commerce add-ins. These add-ins allow you to create a bank account with an online banking system and then purchase items over the Internet without having to send information such as your credit card numbers. After you purchase the items, your electronic account will deduct the amount of the items. Currently, most online electronic commerce, or e-commerce, systems work more like debit systems than credit cards. Therefore, you have to put money in your electronic account before you can purchase items with it.

There are many other add-ins around in addition to those already listed. For example, Adobe offers its Acrobat add-in. Acrobat is a portable document standard that allows any document written with it to be viewed on any computer system that has an Acrobat viewer. Macromedia's Shockwave add-in allows playback of animations created with its product.

6.3.1 VRML

VRML is an extension that has been added to several browsers. VRML stands for Virtual Reality Markup Language. VRML allows HTML pages to be created that allow users to move through and interact with an image on a page. For example, Microsoft provides a VRML page that has their campus on it. Under the image of the campus are buttons that allow the user to move left, right, up, and down. Additionally, users can change the perspective and zoom both in and out of the image.

To use VRML, you must download a VRML add-in for your browser. After you have installed the VRML extension, point your browser at a VRML site to try it out. Look at the home page for whichever browser you have for more information on VRML add-in availability. Here is a sample VRML page reprinted with the permission of Silicon Graphics Incorporated's Cosmo Software (thanks to Andres Wydler!):

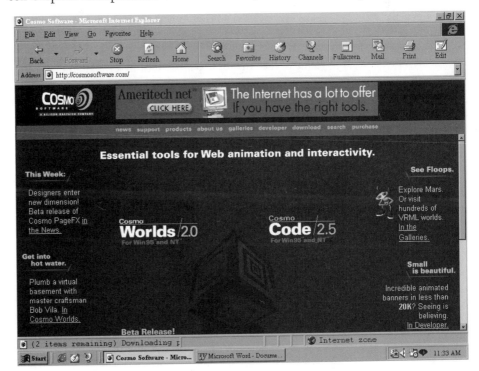

Here are some VRML sites to try out:

http://www.cosmosoftware.com	Cosmo Software's Home Page
http://www.cybertown.com	Cybertown
http::/www.paperinc.com/wrls.html	Paper Software Inc.'s Worlds Page
http://www.planet9.com	Planet 9 Studios

6.3.2 Language Add-ins

The last add-in area we will discuss is language add-ins. Since the Internet has expanded in use, there has become a real need to provide a mechanism to run programs through a browser. Many Web pages allow users to fill out entry forms or access databases. The actual interaction between the user and the Web page has to be carried out by some type of program, since Web pages are static HTML documents.

The first Web page applications were written in languages like Perl or C on UNIX systems. These programs were called CGI scripts (CGI stands for Common Gateway Interface). The CGI script allows the user to enter information. CGI then collects the entered information, processes it, and sends back results, if any. The biggest problem with these programs is that it is difficult to get them to work correctly. After all, these languages were not expressly designed for running programs across the Internet.

Sun Microsystems found that its Java language was well suited to writing programs that could run in Internet browsers. These programs are called applets. Today, most browsers provide support for Javascript. Java is covered in detail in Chapter 8.

Microsoft did not want to be outdone by Sun, so it produced Visual Basic Script, or VB Script, which is a language similar to Javascript. Microsoft felt that since there were already many Visual Basic programmers around, many people might prefer to use this language instead of learning Java. Currently, only Microsoft's Internet Explorer can process Visual Basic Script programs.

6.4 CHANNELS

One of the current hot spots in browser technology is the concept of a *channel*. To use a channel, you simply subscribe to it. (There is no cost involved for most channels.) You can then set up your computer so that whenever you launch the browser, it will go out and retrieve the newest copy of the channel's material for you to use. Many people also set up the browser so that it downloads channels during a time when the user is not around, such as at lunch or in the middle of the night.

The concept of channels are similar to the idea of UseNet News. Most channels pertain to a specific topic or area and provide timely information on that topic. Almost all of the new Internet browsers provide some type of channel mechanism, and many of the large Web sites provide channel services. Here is an example of a channel page from Microsoft Internet Explorer 4.0:

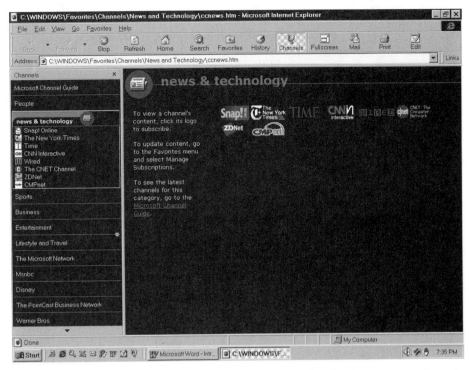

From this screen, I can click on any of the news and technology icons in the right-hand frame to access that particular channel. You can see that the Web pages of companies such as Time, CNN, and Wired are available from this page.

6.5 A LAST RESORT TO ACCESSING THE WEB

If you have a desperate need to try out the Web and don't have any other way to access it, there are a few public Web browser sites that can be telneted to. These sites run an incredibly poor text-based Web browser, but nevertheless, they put you on the web. The text-based browsers are most likely either *lynx* or *www*.

U.S. Public Text WWW Browsers by State:

KS	*ukanaix.cc.ukans.edu*	(login as kufacts)
NJ	*www.njit.edu*	(login as www)
NC	*www.unc.edu*	(login as lynx)
NY	*fatty.law.cornell.edu*	(login as www)

Here are the commands you will need:

Text-Based Lynx and WWW Commands:

Command	Full Name	Description
	number	Follow the specified link
b	back	Jump to previous document in recall list
bo	bottom	Jump to the end of the current document
f *words*	find *words*	Use specified keywords to search index
g *UDL*	go *UDL*	Jump to specified document or resource
h	help	Display command summary and technical info
ho	home	Jump to the starting document
l	list	Display a list of links within current document
m	manual	Jump to the browser reference document
n	next	Jump to the next link within the last document
p	previous	Jump to the previous link within the last document
q	quit	Quit the web
r	recall	Display list of previously visited documents
r *number*	recall *number*	Jump to specified document from the recall list
-	RETURN	Display next screenful of information
t	top	Jump to the beginning of the current document
u	up	Display previous screenful of current document

I suggest that you avoid using this method of Web access. Getting your own Web browser to work is worth the effort that it takes! Text-based public WWW sites provide an extremely poor taste of what the web has to offer.

Here is an example of the IMSE department's home page as viewed with lynx:

```
IMSE at KETTERING   (p1 of 3)


                    Welcome To The IMSE Home Page
                                   at
                          Kettering University




                 Page is constantly being updated.

        _____


          [1]About Industrial & Maufacturing Engineering

             [2]Undergraduate Catalog 1994 - 1995

          [3]Manufacturing Systems Engineering Curriculum

             [4]Industrial Engineering Curriculum
```

```
-- press space for next page --
  Arrow keys: Up and Down to move. Right to follow a link; Left to
  go back.
  H)elp O)ptions P)rint G)o M)ain screen Q)uit /=search
  [delete]=history list
```

SUMMARY

This chapter has introduced what many people consider to be the Internet: the World Wide Web. The chapter has looked at text and graphical browsers. Much of the chapter has been devoted to examining the creation of HTML pages. The chapter has concluded with a look at some of the newer aspects of the web.

KEY TERMS

Add-Ins	HTTP	Tags
Browsers	Hypertext	URL
Channels	Images	VRML
Cookies	Links	Web Server
Home Pages	lynx	World Wide Web
HTML	Search Engines	www

Problems

1. Use your browser to point to http://www.yahoo.com. Print out this page.
2. Use any one of the search engines mentioned in the chapter. Search for stereolithography. Print out the list of sites found.
3. Create an HTML page that has your name, your class, and your instructor's name on it. Print out a copy of the page.
4. Modify the page created in Problem 3 so that you have a horizontal line above and below your name. Print out a copy of the page.
5. Create an HTML page that has some text elements formatted with the following attributes: bold, italics, heading 2, underline and blockquotes. Print out this page.
6. Create an HTML page which has a bulleted list with the four seasons of the year on it. Print out this page.
7. Modify the HTML page created in Problem 6 so that each of the four bullets on the original list has a sublist of two items that you like about each season. Print out this page.
8. Create an HTML page that has your name on it. Insert any graphic that you like (or one suggested by your instructor). Print out a copy of the page.
9. Create two separate HTML pages. Create a text link from one page to the other. Test the pages to ensure that the link works. Print out a copy of the two pages.
10. Modify one of the two text links in Problem 9 so that it is a graphic link. Print out the two pages.

7

Live Communications on the Internet

SCIENCE/ENGINEERING SPOTLIGHT: BARCODE TECHNOLOGIES

You probably do not think much about those little bar codes at the bottom of grocery items. How about the lines at the bottom of the address labels on your mail? Have you seen those weird squares that look like a psychologist's ink-blot test on these labels? All of these patterns are barcodes. Barcodes are an amazing innovation in the tracking of packages. Barcodes no longer have to be one dimensional, like the UPC labels on food items. Two-dimensional barcodes have been created to allow even more information to be stored in a small area. Barcodes allow efficient sorting of items to take place accurately at very high rates of speed and without much human intervention.

SECTIONS

OBJECTIVES

After reading this chapter, you should be able to:

- Name several "chat" programs
- Explain how companies are using live communication on the web

For all of the other Internet services that we have looked at, we examined screens containg what people had written, posted, or sent in the past. However, the Internet provides for live "real-time" communications as well. We will examine the two main types of this kind of communication service: Talk and IRC. The chapter will conclude with an examination of the future of real-time communications and the extensions that have been created for them on the World Wide Web.

7.1 THE TALK PROGRAM

Talk is a program that exists on many UNIX systems. (It has other names on different computers—i.e., DEC's VAX/VMS *phone* command.) Talk tries to locate another user that you specify, and if that user is logged in, it notifies the user that you wish to talk to him or her. The conversation typed by each party then appears in its own window on the screen; thus, talk is entirely text based and is like a telephone conversation int that both parties can "speak" and "hear" simultaneously.

Let us look at an example of talk in which I try to talk to a user named *bjames*, but that user is not logged in on my local system at the time.

```
defiant{sjames}11% talk bjames
---------------------------------------------------------------

[No connection yet]
[Your party is not logged on]




---------------------------------------------------------------
```

That request did not work, but now user *dougj* is requesting to talk with me. I can answer him by typing `talk dougj@nova.kettering.edu`. Notice that this user is not on the same system that I am on; although we both are at Kettering, however, he could be using the Internet on the other side of the world and I would still be able to talk with him.

```
defiant{sjames}12%

Message from Talk_Daemon@defiant at 11:49 ...
talk: connection requested by dougj@nova.kettering.edu.
talk: respond with:  talk dougj@nova.kettering.edu

talk dougj@nova.kettering.edu
---------------------------------------------------------------

[No connection yet]
[Connection established]
```

```
Yes?
```

```
----------------------------------------------------------------
```

```
Just wanted to see what you were up to!
```

```
Talk with you later!
```

```
----------------------------------------------------------------
```

My side of the conversation (what I type) appears in the lower window and what the other user types appears in the upper window. When either person wants to quit the talk facility, all he or she has to do is press *CONTROL-c*.

This particular version of talk will let only two people communicate at once. However, there are also multiple-party talk versions, such as *ntalk, otalk,* and *ytalk.* You might want to try using the *finger* command before requesting to talk with someone to see if your party is logged in.

PRACTICE!

Find out if there is a talk or phone program available to you. Learn how to use this program to communicate with other people on your local system. You may find this program to be an invaluable tool to quickly contact friends and professors in other buildings or rooms when you have a question or need help.

7.2 IRC: INTERNET RELAY CHAT

IRC is the Internet equivalent of the chat rooms that are located on popular Bulletin Board Systems (BBS). The idea behind BBS chat rooms is that someone creates a chat room dedicated to a specific subject, and people who are online can enter the chat room and join in on the conversation. The basic idea of IRC is the sames, except the people who can enter the chat room are those with IRC access on the Internet.

You will find that IRC is a much more chaotic form of conversation than UseNet or e-mail. This is because the people who are on a given *channel* (IRCspeak for a chat room) are all communicating extemporaneously in real time, so the result is like a rambling conversation than the well-thought-out messages that are posted on the other Internet services we have discussed.

The advantages of IRC are that it is free, there are no limits on the number or types of channels that are active, and there is no limit to the number of people who can participate at any given time.

7.2.1 Running IRC

To run IRC, you must either run an IRC client program on your computer or telnet to an IRC provider. If you have an IRC program on your system and you need to supply it with an IRC server to use, here are a few addresses:

IRC Servers by State:

irc.netsys.com   CA

irc.caltech.edu	CA
irc.indiana.edu	IN
csa.bu.edu	MA
wpu.wpi.edu	MA
irc.tc.umn.edu	MN
mothra.syr.edu	NY

If you want to use telnet to gain access to public IRC clients, here are some available hosts:

Public IRC Clients:

wildcar.ecn.uoknor.edu 6667

vinson.ecn.uoknor.edu 6667

sci.dixie.edu 6667

bradenville.andrew.cmu.edu

santafe.santafe.edu (login: *irc*)

7.2.2 Using IRC

Once you have connected to an IRC site, you can start accessing different channels. You may first want to pick a nickname. If you do not pick one, your username will be used by default. Nicknames make IRC more personal and fun and accommodate those users who have meaningless and/or numeric usernames.

If you do pick a nickname, here are few tips for doing so:

- Stay with one nickname, do not change it.
- Keep the nickname simple, and do not use special characters.
- Nicknames are limited to nine characters in length.

To set your nickname, type */NICK nickname_you_want*. Here is a sample of an IRC screen:

```
*** - 30/6/1996 21:19
*** - Welcome to the NetOne(tm) IRC Server
*** -
*** - Appropriate Language and Behavior are mandatory.
*** -
*** - User Bots are not allowed on Channel #NetOne.
*** -
*** - Report problems to Milkman (tlyon) or Lane (lane), your IRC Operator.
*** -
*** - Thanks for joining us, we're glad you're here.
*** -
*** End of /MOTD command.
*** Channel      Users  Topic
*** #other       1
*** #netone      3      Ahh, Sleep... Sleep is the only Adventure.
*** #cyberpsychos    2      Giant insects wearing plaid linoleum negliges
*** End of /LIST
*** sjames (sjames@defiant.kettering.edu) has joined channel #netone
*** Topic for #netone: Ahh, Sleep... Sleep is the only Adventure.
*** The topic was set by jeff 29732 sec ago
*** Users on #netone: sjames gutz @Ventrue_AFK @VCSBot
```

```
*** Channel #netone was created at Fri Aug  9 08:14:42 1996
 12:23PM [1] sjames #netone (M: 2)  ircII2.8.2-EPIC3 -- Type /help for help
>
```

">", on the last line, is where you type in all IRC commands.

How do you find the channels that are available to join? Use the /LIST command. /LIST shows every channel that is available. This list could be quite large.

All channels start with the pound (#) sign. Even if someone refers to a channel without providing the # sign, you still must type it in when accessing that channel. This character is how we separate the users' names from the channels.

To join a channel, type /JOIN #channel. Once you have joined a channel, anything you type will appear to all users of the channel, with your nickname in brackets next to what you type. The bracketed nickname is used to let the other users of the channel know who types what.

To leave a channel, type /LEAVE #channel or /PART #channel.

There is help available on IRC if you type /HELP or /HELP command. If I want to know what the /LIST command does, for example, I could type /HELP list.

To find out who is on a channel, use the /WHO command. This command will list the nicknames of all the people on the channel. For each user that is on the channel, you will see a status value: <u>A</u> indicates that the user is away from his or her machine at the moment, <u>H</u> indicates that the user is on his or her machine and active using IRC at the time, ° indicates that the user is an *IRCop* (an IRC operator), and @ indicates that the user is a ChanOp (channel operator).

If you need to leave IRC for a minute, you can inform other users with the /AWAY command. For example typeing /AWAY causes I'll be back in a minute to appear on everyone else's screen. You will receive a reply letting you know that you were marked as away. To deactivate the away status, just type /AWAY again.

The other user-related commands that provide information on channel users are /WHOIS which tells who is currently on the channel and /WHOWAS, which tells who was on the channel.

If you are annoyed by the messages that certain users are typing, you can ignore them via the /IGNORE command. The typical format of the /IGNORE command is /IGNORE nickname option. *Option* could be <u>ALL</u> (ignore all messages from this user), <u>NONE</u> (ignore none of this user's messages), <u>MSG</u> (ignore only private messages sent with /MSG), <u>NOTICE</u> (ignore only private messages sent with /NOTICE), and <u>INVITE</u> (ignores channel invites from the user). If you enter /IGNORE without the nickname or option, it will list all of the people you are ignoring and which option(s) you have set for each.

Personal conversations can be carried out on any IRC channel. The /MSG command allows you to send a message to one or more specific users. The format is /MSG usernickname1 text. You may specify multiple usernames separated by commas.The recipients of the message will see your nickname in asterisks to indicate that the message they just received is private, as opposed to one of the usual bracketed public messages. /NOTICE is a command that is identical in nature to /MSG, except that hyphens are used in place of the asterisks.

If you want to send a fairly long private communication, you should use the /QUERY command, which allows you to type a long message. To start the /QUERY command, type /QUERY usernickname. At this point, you can enter your message. When you are finished, type /QUERY.

If security reasons prompt you to want to send encrypted messages, IRC provides a method by which you may do so. Say that users *sjames* and *dblasdell* want to send encrypted messages to each other. They must agree on a common password for this procedure: in this case, say they agree on the password *nova:*.

User *sjames* first types:

```
/ENCRYPT dblasdell nova
```

User *dblasdell* then types:

```
/ENCRYPT sjames nova
```

Now the messages between users *sjames* and *dblasdell* will be encrypted, and only they can see the unencrypted message. Everyone else would receive an [ENCRYPTED MESSAGE] notice.

Other Miscellaneous IRC Commands

* If you want to review any past text, type the command */LASTLOG lines_to_ review*. If you want to view messages from only one user, use the */LASTLOG nickname [-Public] lines_to_review* command. If the *-Public* option is used, it shows only the messages sent from *nickname* to everyone on the channel.
* To create your own channel, just type */JOIN #newchannelname*. You might want to set the channel mode by */MODE °channel* or *nickname° +options*.

Available Channel Options

i	Users must be invited to join
l<number>	Only a certain number of users can be on at once
m	Only people with operator privileges can talk
n	*/MSGs* from outside the channel are not allowed
p	The channel is private
s	The channel is secret (it doesn't show up in /LIST command)
t	Only channel operators can change the channel's topic

Available User Options

in	Make yourself invisible
o	IRC-operator status
s	Allows you to receive server messages

7.2.3 One Final Note: IRCbots

IRCbots are automated programs set up by IRC users to perform certain tasks over IRC. IRCbots are often seen as wasteful and annoying—i.e., the Barneybot, which sings the Barney theme song. IRCbots are basically programs that IRC users can interact; examples include a joke bot, bartender bot, poetry bot, and so forth. Only a few servers allow the use of IRC bots.

7.3 THE FUTURE OF LIVE COMMUNICATIONS

If the concept of real-time text conversation has enchanted you, you will be pleased to know that there are a few real-time voice programs available. One of the programs, InternetPhone, allow users of computers with audio capabilities to join an IRC channel and audibly talk over the Internet. You speak through your computer's microphone to other users across the world, and you hear their replies over the computer's speakers.

This program is as close as you can get to having free worldwide long-distance phone calls, since you do not directly pay for these calls. Another audio facility, VoiceChat, just requires TCP/IP capabilities for users of two multimedia computers to talk to one another without having to resort to IRC.

Many of these types of programs are available both as stand-alone programs and as add-ins for Internet browsers. For more information on add-ins, see Chapter 6.

7.3.1 RealAudio

If the thoughts of talking to someone over real time has interested you, how would you like the ability to listen to music, sports, and talk shows over real time on your computer? *RealAudio*, by Progressive Networks (*http://www.realaudio.com*), allows real-time transmissions of audio material to be sent over the Internet.

RealAudio is an add-in that is available for a number of browsers. Once you have installed a copy of RealAudio, point it at the following sites to see what it can do:

ABC RadioNet	http://www.abcradionet.com
C/Net Radio	http://www.cnet.com/Content/Radio/index.html
ESPN SportsZone	http://espnet.sportszone.com
National Public Radio	http://www.realaudio.com/contentp.npr

Here's what Progressive Networks, Inc. RealAudio home page looks like (Thanks to Jenny Sorensen, Mark Lewis, et. al.):

Copyright© 1995–1997 Real Networks, Inc., 1111 Thrid Avenue, Suite 2900, Seattle, Washington 98101 U.S.A. All rights reserved. RealNetworks, RealAudio, RealVideo, RealMedia, RealPlayer, and other names or logos are trademarks or registered trademarks of RealNetworks, Inc.

7.3.2 StreamWorks

Audio is not the only item that is available on demand over the Internet. Video feeds are available too. Xing Technologies' StreamWorks (*http://www.xingtech.com*) is a browser add-in that handles both audio and video feeds.

The following is a list of some Xing broadcasting sites:

Bloomberg News Radio	http://www.bloomberg.com/	audio/
	cgi-bin/tdisp.sh?wbbr/index.html	video
iRock Radio	http://www.irock.com	audio
KMPS, Seattle	http://www.kmps.com	audio
KPIG, Santa Cruz	http://www.kpig.com	audio
KZOK, Seattle	http://www.kzok.com	audio
NBC Pro Financial Network	http://www.xingtech.com/nbc.html	video

Here is Xing Technologies Corporation's home page:

Have you ever received a phone call from someone asking you for help with something, and you thought, "If I could just see what's going on there, I could do so much more to help?" With the capabilities of the Internet today, you can see what is going on elsewhere in real time. From conducting video meetings to troubleshooting a problem halfway around the world, all it takes is some software and a video camera. There are several video sites on the Internet that provide snapshots of what is happening at a given site in real time.

I have access to a camera inside the Computer-Integrated Manufacturing (CIM) laboratory at Kettering University. With it, I can allow other people to see what is going on inside the laboratory in real time through a browser. In other words, I can broadcast images of machines in operation without requiring people even to step into the lab to see these processes. This same technology allows me to broadcast images of broken or malfunctioning equipment to manufacturers to permit them to see what is going on with the equipment before they make a service call. The next set of images is from the CIM laboratory at Kettering University. (Thanks to Dr. Steve Aylor of the IMSE Department at Kettering for the images!)

The first image shows a robotic cell. Two robots can interact in the same workspace and pick and place workpieces that arrive to the cell by the plastic palette in the middle of the picture.

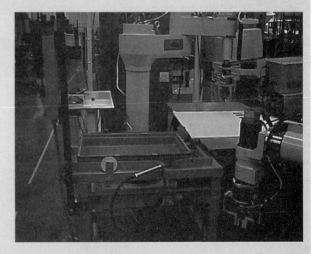

The next image shows one of our manufacturing cells. This particular work cell has a robot that can load and unload workpieces from the N/C (numerically controlled) vertical milling center located behind it.

 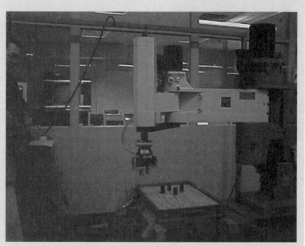

The last image from the CIM laboratory shows a Kettering student programming a robot to perform a palletizing application. In this case, the robot is to remove pegs from the wooden palette and then drop the pegs off at another location.

The intergration of video input with the Internet has just started to open up exciting possibilities like those previously mentioned. For example, many colleges are examining the possibilities of providing distance-learning classes through the use of the Internet. With a camera mounted at both the student's location and the teacher's location, classes may be offered in this manner.

PRACTICE!

Point your browser to *http://www.computersamerica.com/mousing_around/gatecam/* for a look at the Golden Gate bridge in San Francisco. To find more video output on the Internet, use a search engine to search for "Internet camera".

The following Web page picture is courtesy of ComputerAmerica.com (Thanks to Joe Ules):

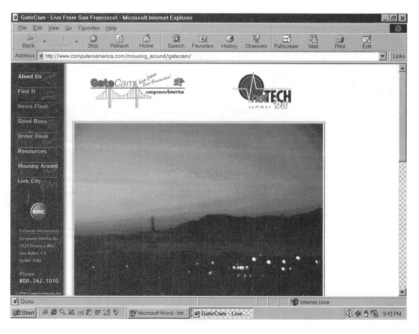

SUMMARY   This chapter has looked at real-time communications on the Internet. Two text-based programs that allow users to chat with one another have been examined: talk and IRC. The chapter has concluded with a look at the future of communications on the Internet for such communications, both audio and video output can be transferred to computers that are equipped to receive the transmissions.

KEY TERMS

Channel	IRCop	StreamWorks
IRC	Nicknames	Talk
IRCbots	RealAudio	

Problems

1. Determine if your institution has a "talk" or "phone" command. If it does, try using it to converse with a friend.
2. Access IRC and join a group or two. Write up a summary of your impression of IRC.
3. Determine if your browser supports RealAudio. If it does, listen to and report on the top stories from ABC RadioNet, located at *http://www.abcradionet.com*.
4. Determine if your browser supports Stream Works. If it does, check out what is happening on the NBC Pro Financial Network, located at *http://www.xingtech.com/nbc.html*.

8

Java

SCIENCE/ENGINEERING SPOTLIGHT: ARTIFICIAL INTELLIGENCE

As computers get faster, the amount of processing that computers can perform greatly increases. One of the areas of computer science that can most benefit by this increase in speed is artificial intelligence (AI). Artificial intelligence is the ability for a computer system to make decisions intelligently, or even to "learn."

There are several branches of AI. On one hand, there are expert systems, which capture the knowledge of an expert within a given area. When a user interacts with the expert system, the computer interactively works with the user to get information and then makes decisions or recommendations based on that information. An example of this type of system is a medical expert system. Software and knowledge engineers gather information on how a doctor makes a diagnosis and then build that knowledge into the expert system. When a user works with this expert system, the system might begin by asking the user things such as "Are you running a fever?", "How long have you been coughing?", and so forth. This method is similar to the way that a doctor analyzes the symptoms a patient describes. After enough information has been gathered from the patient, the expert system may be able to offer a diagnosis.

OBJECTIVES

After reading this chapter, you should be able to:

- Describe Java's history and who created it
- Explain what an applet is
- Write a basic programming loop in JAVA
- Write your own applet

Another area of AI is neural networks. A neural network is a computer application that uses inputs and learns from the importance of those inputs. This process is very similar to how the human mind works. Think about how many times you have put your hand on a hot stove before you learned that it hurts to do so. A neural network learns in much the same way. Neural networks have been used to perform diverse tasks, such as weather forecasting and stock-market predictions.

The future of AI continues to get brighter as computers get faster, since many more decisions can be made in a short amount of time. It will not be too long before you will be able to speak to a computer and have it respond correctly through the use of artificially intelligent voice recognition.

8.1 INTRODUCTION TO JAVA

Java is a computer programming language designed by Sun Microsystems. Java was written for a project internal to Sun. The developers started the project in C++, but quickly realized that there was a need for a better, stronger language that would run across multiple platforms with no required change. The original use for Java never came to fruition, however, and consequently, Java sat on a shelf for a period of time.

Enter the Internet! As the Internet expanded, it became obvious that there needed to be a way to write interactive Web pages. Internet users were not going to be satisfied with just looking at static text pages. Users needed to be able to input information into a Web page and immediately get results back, as in the use of a search engine. If electronic commerce was ever going to become a reality, this problem had to be solved.

At the time interactive Web pages were created with languages called *Perl* and *CGI* that ran on UNIX computers only. There were two major limitations with this approach: 1) Perl and CGI were not the easiest languages to work with. Writing complicated Web scripts was very difficult with them. 2) Not everybody was running UNIX, so not everybody could create Web pages.

One of the major premises behind Java was that it should be able to run on any computer capable of running a Java Virtual Machine (JVM). The Java Virtual Machine is essentially a piece of software that can execute Java programs. JVMs are available for just about every type of computer that is used today: Macintosh, PC, UNIX workstations, etc.

The other powerful feature of Java that enhanced its use on the Internet is that it is platform independent. Java does not require a specific microprocessor to run; all it requires is a JVM. (Obviously, the JVM must be able to run on the hardware, though.) If you write a Java program, it can run on any computer that has a JVM. This feature is similar to the concept of a browser: If you can get a browser for your computer, you can view Web pages. Java thereby became the vehicle of choice for writing programs to be executed across the Internet through a browser interface.

Java offers several wonderful programming features:

- Java will not allow Java applets to write directly to your hard drive. This feature helps to contain the spread of computer viruses and other malicious code.
- Java fully embraces the Internet; network support is a core component of Java.
- Many of the bad language features of C and C++ have been eliminated in Java, making it easier for new programmers to learn object-oriented programming than ever before.

Java is one of the hotspots of Internet development today. This chapter will examine what is needed to write Java programs and how to write some basic Java applets and applications. Not every facet of the Java language will be examined in this chapter, since completely covering the Java language would require a book far greater in size than this one.

8.2 REQUIREMENTS TO USE JAVA

If you only want to use Java programs contained within Web pages, all you need is a Java-enabled Web browser. Microsoft's Internet Explorer, Netscape's Navigator, and Sun's HotJava browser can all do this.

If you want to write Java programs, then you need to get a Java compiler. A compiler is a piece of software that converts a computer program written in a specific language into a program that the computer can run. Almost every software application that you use was written in some computer language, like Java, C++, C, Fortran, Pascal, Basic, etc. A computer cannot directly run this program; instead, the source-code program must be converted into an executable program. Executable programs are binary files that are in the computer's "native tongue."

There are many Java compilers available today. Some are commercial Java programs like Microsoft's Visual J++, and others are free, such as Sun's Java SDK (Software Development Kit). If you want to write Java programs, you must have one of these compilers installed on your computer. This chapter assumes that you have some type of Java compiler available for use and that you have learned what is required to enter and compile Java programs.

8.3 APPLETS VS. APPLICATIONS

There are two very different types of Java programs that can be written. *Applets* are Java programs that are designed to run within another program. All of the Java programs that are executed from within your Web browser are applets. On the other hand, Java can create complete programs that are stand-alone in nature. These types of Java programs are called *applications*.

Let us start this section by taking a look at how to create a Java program of each type. This section will briefly discuss what Java code does and then explain how it works at the end of the section.

How you enter your program depends a great deal on which Java compiler you are using. Your instructor or computer-center staff should be able to help you find information on the compiler you will be using. If you are installing a Java compiler on your own computer, there are usually detailed examples and instructions included in the manual to get you started. Type in the Java program that follows and save it under your compiler as AppletSample. This applet will simply print out a message when it is run from within a browser.

```
import java.applet.Applet;
import java.awt.Graphics;

public class AppletSample extends Applet

{
    String AString;
```

```
public void init()

{
        AString = new String("This is my first Applet");
        show();

}

public void paint(Graphics gfx)

{
        gfx.drawString(AString, 30, 60);
}
}
```

Make sure that you follow all punctuation carefully, and do not change the case of any of the letters. If you make any errors, this applet will not compile correctly.

Once you have successfully typed in and compiled your applet, you should be able to create a Web page that runs your applet within it. I am using Microsoft Visual J++ for these examples, and it does all of the work automatically. Here is the applet running from within my browser:

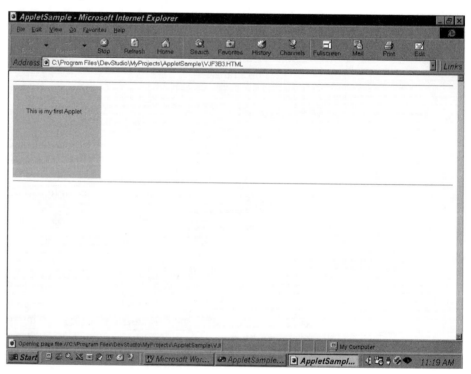

Here is what the page's HTML code looks like:

```
<html>
<head>
<title>AppletSample</title>
</head>
<body>
<hr>
<applet
```

```
code=AppletSample
width=200
height=200>

</applet>
<hr>
</body>
</html>
```

Notice that toward the end of the HTML code, there is a section we have not previously encountered: applet. In this case, the name of the code is set to AppletSample, which is what we called our applet. The applet is to run with a width and height of 200 pixels (picture element) each. As you can see, it is quite simple to add a Java applet to a Web page. The tough part is getting the applet to compile correctly first.

Now let us create a Java application that will ask a user for three numbers and then print out the average of those three numbers. Save this file under ApplicationSample.

```
import java.io.*;

public class ApplicationSample

{
      public static void main(String args[])
            throws IOException

      {
      int num1,num2,num3;
      double ave;
      BufferedReader stdin = new
            BufferedReader(new InputStreamReader(System.in));

      System.out.println("This program will average three
numbers");
      System.out.println("Enter your first number:");
      num1 = Integer.parseInt(stdin.readLine());
      System.out.println("Enter your second number:");
      num2 = Integer.parseInt(stdin.readLine());
      System.out.println("Enter your third number:");
      num3 = Integer.parseInt(stdin.readLine());
      ave = (num1 + num2 + num3) / 3.0;
      System.out.print("Your numbers average out to "+ave);
      }
}
```

Notice that when the application executes, it just goes to a basic text window:

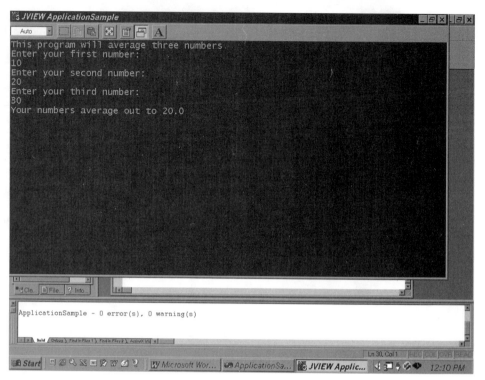

These examples are not particularly interesting or complex, but you should have a good idea of the difference between a Java applet and a Java application at this point. Now, let us go back and take a look at the Java code to understand how it works. Here are the first two lines of the code:

```
import java.applet.*;
import java.awt.*;
```

The first two lines of the applet tell the Java compiler which packages to include. A package is a collection of routines that are related. A math package might have the square-root, exponential, logarithmic, and trignometric functions contained inside of it. The *applet* package includes the support routines necessary for transforming this code into something that can be run from within a browser. The *awt* (*Abstract Window Toolkit*) package contains all of the functions related to displaying and interacting with graphical interfaces, which is what a browser is. Now let us examine the next line of the code.

```
public class AppletSample extends Applet
```

This line identifies that we are creating a new class called AppletSample, which is the name of our applet, and that it extends the *Applet* class. In other words, we are going to create a new applet. The word *public* means that everything will be able to see and call our AppletSample. The next line denotes the start of a block of code.

```
{
```

The next line creates a variable called *AString*. A variable is a piece of data whose value can change while the program is running. Program *variables* are very similar to variables in mathematical functions, such as x in $f(x) = 5x + 2x$. Notice that the variable x can take on many different values.

```
String AString;
```

The next lines create a function called *init*. This function is called whenever the applet gets started up. In this case, the *init* function places the value "This is my first Applet" inside of the *AString* variable. The *init* function then calls the *show* routine, which displays the window where the applet will run.

```
public void init()

{
        AString = new String("This is my first Applet");
        show();

}
```

The next lines invoke the *paint* function. This function gets called when the applet window needs to be updated. In our applet, we want the string we created to be printed in the window. The *drawString* function allows us to do that. The values 30 and 60 refer to the *x*-and *y*-coordinates of the location where the string should be printed within the applet window.

```
public void paint(Graphics gfx)

{
        gfx.drawString(AString, 30, 60);
}
```

Last, but not least, we need to close the block that we started after the *public class AppletSample* line:

```
}
```

The application that we wrote has some similarities to the applet. Let us take a look at the application code.

First, I need to include the *java.io* package so that I can read from the keyboard.

```
import java.io.*;
```

The next line signals that we are going to create an application called *Application-Sample*. Notice that this line does not say anything about applets or extending applets.

```
public class ApplicationSample

{
```

The first function that we run across inside of the ApplicationSample class is *main*. All applications will begin executing at the main function, and when the end of the *main* function is reached, the application will stop executing. The *public static* part of the next line simply says that anyone who wants to use *main* will be able to see it. *Static* is a special modifier that says *main* will be created once and exist for the whole duration of the program's execution. This feature ensures that there can only be one *main* function in any given application.

The *String args[]* expression inside of the parentheses following *main* indicate that this function has the ability to receive a set of strings. In this case, the strings would come from the operating system. For example, when you type the command *rename file1.dat file2.dat*, all of this information is sent into the *rename* program, where the program can figure out what is to be renamed.

The *throws IOException* expression identifies that if the *main* function encounters an error, it can throw an error, which means that Java provides a way to handle errors so that they do not crash the program and then bring the user back to the operating system.

```
public static void main(String args[])
        throws IOException

{
```

The next set of statements declares variables. You can see that the first three are called *num1, num2,* and *num3*. These variables are all of type *integer*, meaning that they hold whole numbers. The second line creates a variable by the name of *ave* that holds a number of type *double* (a number with a decimal point). Finally, the third line creates a variable called *stdin* that is set up to read information from the keyboard. The line after the equals (=) sign signals the program to read information input through the keyboard. We will learn more details about the syntax after the = sign in the next section.

```
int num1,num2,num3;
double ave;
BufferedReader stdin = new
        BufferedReader(new InputStreamReader(System.in));
```

From here, the program is actually quite simple. The *System.out.println* statements in the next set of lines write information to the screen. The program starts up by telling the user what the program is used for and then asks the user for the first number. The *Integer.parseInt(stdin.readLine())* routine reads a line from the keyboard and then converts it into an integer. The result from the conversion is placed into variable *num1*.

```
System.out.println("This program will average three
numbers");
    System.out.println("Enter your first number:");
    num1 = Integer.parseInt(stdin.readLine());
```

The same basic task of prompting the user for a number and then reading it in from the keyboard is repeated to get the second and third numbers:

```
System.out.println("Enter your second number:");
num2 = Integer.parseInt(stdin.readLine());
System.out.println("Enter your third number:");
num3 = Integer.parseInt(stdin.readLine());
```

Since we now have all three of our numbers, we can do some math to calculate the average and then print that information out to the user:

```
ave = (num1 + num2 + num3) / 3.0;
System.out.println("Your numbers average out to "+ave);
}
}
```

PRACTICE!

Before continuing in this section, make sure that you can enter both the application and applet presented. Make sure that you know how to compile them and get them to execute.

8.4 BASICS OF THE JAVA LANGUAGE

This section of the chapter will introduce you to some of the basics of the Java language. This section is by no means an exhaustive or in-depth view of the topics, but rather, it serves as a foundation from which you can begin to experiment and develop basic Java applications.

8.4.1 Comments

Comments allow you to describe what is going on inside of your Java programs. Comments do not actually get compiled, so they do not slow your programs down. They are very valuable in assisting those reading the source code to determine what each segment of program code does. Comments are placed after two // (slash marks). Everything on a line after the // marks is assumed to be a comment. For example,

```
//The next line will declare the parts of a user's name
String FName,MName,LName;
```

8.4.2 Variables

We have already said that variables are reserved areas where we can place data items. The data items placed inside of variables can change while the program is running. Declaring variables is easy; you simply preface the variable name with the type of data that the variable is to store. Java provides eight basic data types to choose from:

Type	Name	Purpose
Integer	int	Stores whole numbers in the range + -/ 2,147,483,647
Short	short	Stores whole numbers in the range + -/ 32,767
Long	long	Stores whole numbers in the range + -/ 9,223,372,036,854,775,807
Byte	byte	Stores whole numbers in the range + -/ 127
Float	float	Stores numbers with decimal points in the range + -/ 3.4E+38 (7 significant digits)
Double	double	Stores numbers with decimal points in the range + -/ 1.8E+308 (15 significant digits)
Character	char	Stores a single character enclosed in single quotes
Boolean	boolean	Can hold either the value *true* or the value *false*

Variables names cannot be the same as any reserved Java word and must start with a letter. After the initial letter, variable names can include other letters, numbers, the underscore sign and the dollar sign. Variable names are case sensitive. Here are some examples of variable declarations:

```
int x,y;           //Creates two variables of type integer
float money;       //Creates one variable of type float
```

Values can be assigned to variables through the use of the assignment statement, which is the equals (=) sign. Here are some examples of how we assign values to variables:

```
x = 5;             //Puts the value 5 in the variable x
y = -7;
money = 23.54;
```

8.4.3 Basic Operators in Java

Java includes several different operators for performing math and incrementing and decrementing variables. The following list shows each operator and its respective purpose:

Operator	Purpose
+	Performs addition
-	Performs subtraction
*	Performs multiplication
/	Performs division
%	Returns the modulus remainder from integer division
++	Increments a variable's value by 1
--	Decrements a variable's value by 1
Math.pow(x,y)	Raises x to the y power (inside the Math package)

Examples of the use of these operators include:

```
int intA1,intA2,intA3;
float floatB1,floatB2,floatB3;

intA1 = 2;
intA2 = 3;
intA3 = intA1 * intA2; //intA3 now has 6 in it
intA3 = intA2 / intA1; //intA3 now has 1 in it due to integer
                       // division
                       // 2 goes into 3 evenly 1 time with a
                       // remainder
                       // of 1
intA3 = intA2 % intA1; //the remainder would be 1

floatB1 = 10.0;
floatB2 = 5.0;
floatB3 = floatB2 / floatB1; //floatB3 would have 0.5 in it

intA1++;          //increments A1 by 1, from 2 to 3
intA2--;          //decrements A2 by 1, from 3 to 2
```

8.4.4 Strings

Strings are another type of data that is available with Java. Strings are groups of characters that are related in some way, such as the characters in a person's name. Strings are not one of the basic variable types, and consequently, they work a little differently than do the types of variables we have previously discussed.

You can create variables of type *String* and assign values to the variable through use of the assignment operator. One difference between strings and characters are that strings require their contents to be enclosed in double quotes rather than the single quotes that characters use. Here are some examples of strings:

```
String Message = "Hi There!";//Declares a string and puts a
                             // value in
String Name = "";            //This string is empty
String Fname = "John";
String Lname = "Dough";
String Achunk;
```

```
//Let's concatenate the name strings together into Name
Name = Fname + " " + Lname;   //Name = "John Dough"
```

8.4.5 Basic Program Output with the Println Statement

At this point, we have examined how to create variables, work with their contents, and perform basic operations. We have not considered how to write out any information or output from our programs. This task is actually quite easy with the *print* and *println* statements.

Both statements write to the screen whichever values are enclosed inside of the statement's parentheses. The main difference between the *print* statement and the *println* statement is that the *println* statement goes to a new line after writing its contents, whereas the *print* statement stays on the same line after writing.

The user may send any string to the *print* or *println* statements. The statements are also able to print out any of the basic data types that are built into Java. If you have more than one item to be printed out in the *print* or *println* statement, you can concatenate the information together by using the plus (+) symbol. Some examples of print and println statements are:

```
System.out.println("My name is Sue"); //Prints the message and goes
                                       //  to a new line


System.out.print("one ");
System.out.print(" at ");
System.out.print(" a ");
System.out.println(" time."); //Prints "one at a time" and then goes to
                              //  a new line


System.out.println("I am "+30+" years old"); //Prints "I am 30 years
                                              //  old" and goes to a
                                              //  new line


System.out.println("The answer is "+57.43);  //Prints "The answer is
                                              //  57.43"
```

8.4.6 Making Decisions with the If Statement

Java allows programs to make decisions by using the *if* statement. The basic syntax of the *if* statement is:

```
if (condition)
  {
     execute this if condition is true
  }
else
  {
     execute this if condition is false
  }
```

Most of the time, the condition will consist of one or more of the following conditional operators:

Operator	Purpose
==	is equal to
!=	is not equal to
>	is greater than

>=	is greater than or equal to
<=	is less than or equal to
<	is less than
&&	and operator
||	or operator
!	not operator

Here are some examples of the *if* statement:

```
//This example just prints a message if a is greater than b
int a,b;

a = 10;
b = 5;
if (a > b)
   {
    System.out.println("a is bigger than b");
   }
```

```
//This example just prints out "a is bigger than b" if a is
//greater
//  than b, otherwise the program prints "b is bigger than a"
int a,b;

a = 10;
b = 5;
if (a > b)
   {
    System.out.println("a is bigger than b");
   }
else
   {
    System.out.println("b is bigger than a");
   }
```

```
//This example determines which one is the biggest and prints a
//  message if one variable is greater than the other, or if
//  the variables are equal
int a,b;

a = 10;
b = 5;
if (a > b)
   {
    System.out.println("a is bigger than b");
   }
else
   {
     if (b > a)
       {
```

```
        System.out.println("b is bigger than a");
    }
  else
    {
        System.out.println("a equals b");
    }
}
```

```
//This example will produce an error when trying to compare two
//strings for equality.  The code example then continues with
the
//correct way to perform the comparison.
String Astring = "Yes";
String Bstring = "No";

if (Astring == Bstring) //This produces an error...
                        // you must use the equals operator
                        // built into the string class

if (Astring.compare(Bstring)) //This is the right way to do it
  {
      System.out.println("The strings are equal!");
  }
```

8.4.7 Getting Input from the Keyboard

You might assume that getting input is simple since producing output in Java is so easy. This assumption is not at all true. The easiest way to get input from the keyboard is to point to an *InputStreamReader* at the *System.in* device. The *InputStreamReader* will basically process information sent from the keyboard.

The second requirement is to set up a *BufferedReader*, which processes and holds more than one character at a time from the keyboard. What this process means to you as a programmer is that you will construct the following code:

```
BufferedReader stdin =
        new BufferedReader(new InputStreamReader(System.in));
```

This small line of code has the ability to read anything that the user types in from the keyboard. The resulting information that is typed in will be returned as a string. To convert the information from a string into some other data type, simply use the *parse* or *valueOf* functions built into the appropriate data type.

For example, if I want to convert what a user typed in from a string into an integer, I enter the following line of code, which does the conversion and stores the result in the variable called *num1*:

```
num1 = Integer.parseInt(stdin.readLine());  //num1 must be integer
```

The *parseInt* function is not available for values of type *double*, so we must use the *valueOf* function instead:

```
num3 = Double.valueOf(stdin.readLine());  //num2 must be double
```

PRACTICE!

Let us write a Java application that will calculate the cost of a mortgage payment. The formula to calculate the monthly payment is:

$$\frac{principal \bullet monthly\ interest}{(1 - (1/(1 + monthly\ interest)^{years*12}))} \qquad (8\text{-}1)$$

Here is the Java application code for the calculation:

```java
import java.io.*;

public class Mortgage
{
     public static void Main(String args[]) throws IOException
     {
          Double Principal;
          Double Interest;
          int Years;
          double Monthlyinterest;
          double Payment;

          BufferedReader stdin = new BufferedReader(new
InputStreamReader(System.in));

               //Get the user's information

          System.out.println("Enter your principal amount (no $
or ,):");
          Principal = Double.valueOf(stdin.readLine());
          System.out.println("Enter your interest rate in %:");
          Interest = Double.valueOf(stdin.readLine());
          Interest = Interest/100.0;
          System.out.println("Enter the number of years on the mort-
gage:");
          Years = Integer.parseInt(stdin.readLine());

          //Do the necessary calculations

          Monthlyinterest = Interest / 12.0;
          Payment = Principal * Monthlyinterest /
                         (1.0 - (Math.pow(1.0/(1.0 +
Monthlyinterest),

                                Years * 12.0)));

          //Print the results

          System.out.println("Your payment is "+Payment);
     }
}
```

Test your application against a $10,000 mortgage for 5 years at a 7% interest rate. The application should return a monthly payment value of $198.01.

8.4.8 Loop Structures in Java

Another common programming task that we encounter when writing programs is getting the computer to repeatedly execute a series of instructions. This programming construct is called a loop. With Java, we have three types of loops: *for, while,* and *do-while.*

Here is the basic syntax of the *for* loop:

```
for (initial value;condition;increment)
   {
    instructions to be executed in loop
   }
```

Some examples of the use of the *for* loop are:

```
//print all of the numbers from 1 to 50
for (int j=1;j<=50;j++)

   //The int j=1 is the initial value of j when the loop starts
   //The j<=50 says that the loop will continue executing while
   //   j <= 50
   //The j++ says that j will be incremented by one after each loop
   //   iteration

   {
     System.out.println("Loop is on number "+j);
   }



//This program will print out the basic multiplication table values
for (k=1;k<=12;k++)
   {
     for (l=1;l<=12;l++)
        {
           System.out.println(k+" x "+l+" = "+(k*l));
        }
   }
```

The basic syntax of the *while* loop is:

```
while (condition)
   {
    statements to be executed while the condition is true
   }
```

Some examples of the use of the *while* loop are:

```
//This program will read values from the user while the number that the
// user inputs is positive.  Once the user enters a non-positive number
// the loop will print out what the largest value entered was.

int biggest,input;
BufferedReader stdin = new BufferedReader(new InputStreamReader
(System.in)));

input = 1;
biggest = 0;
while (input > 0)
   {
     System.out.println("Enter a number (non-positive to quit):");
     input = Integer.parseInt(stdin.readLine());
     if (input > biggest)
        {
          biggest = input;
```

```
   }
  }
System.out.println("The biggest number entered was "+biggest);
```

The basic syntax of the *do-while* loop is:

```
do
{
 statements to be executed while the condition is true
}
while (condition)
```

An example of the use of the *do-while* loop is:

```
//This program prints a countdown sequence
int j = 10;

do
  {
    System.out.println(j);
    j--;
  }
while (j>0);
System.out.println("Blastoff!");
```

At this point, you have the fundamental programming background necessary to develop some simple Java applications. You have not been exposed to many of the more complicated topics necessary to fully understand Java, however. You should study topics such as arrays, collections, classes, object-oriented programming, exception handling, threads, network, and JavaBeans before you can say that you are competent in programming with Java. These topics are far outside the scope of this module, but are addressed in a number of excellent books available on Java.

PROFESSIONAL SUCCESS:
DANGER: TAKING THE INTERNET AT FACE VALUE

One of the biggest mistakes that you can make with the Internet is to assume that everything that you run across and encounter is absolutely true. If you are taking a math exam, do you double check your answers? Most likely you do. The reason for doing so is obvious: If there was any error in the calculation, the answer could be severely affected.

Information located on the Internet should be treated in the same way. How do you know that the information is correct? How do you guarantee it? The same questions could be considered if you are getting information from a book. How do you know that the information is accurate? Simply put, you do not. You need to verify the accuracy of the information by checking it against other sources. If several sources seem to concur with the information presented, then, for the most part, you can assume it is fairly accurate.

I have run across student presentations in which the students grabbed information right off of the Internet and placed it into a project without even verifying it. In the best case, bad information may just be misleading and somewhat incorrect. In the worst case, bad information may cause a project to go wildly off track if the project builds upon the data and the data is wrong.

Anytime you are collecting information from the Internet, always be very suspect of its accuracy. Taking the information at face value could be an incredibly big mistake.

8.5 MORE ON APPLETS

In this section, I want to write a couple of new applets and comment on how the applets work. The graphical-and event-based processing required by applets is somewhat difficult to grasp. However, I think that it is worth our time to examine a couple of applets to get a feel for what applets are capable of doing and some of the code encountered in getting the applets to carry out those tasks.

The first applet we are going to write is the TickerTape applet. This applet is a Java classic that you have probably run across on the Internet. The TickerTape applet takes a text message and scrolls it from left to right, inside of a browser. Here is the complete source code for TickerTape, along with comments describing how the program works:

```java
//import both the applet and abstract window toolkit packages

import java.applet.*;
import java.awt.*;

//Here's the applet header
public class TickerTape extends Applet implements Runnable
{

        Thread TTapeThread = null;    //Create this as a thread
        boolean Suspended = true;     //Indicates if applet is running
        String TextMessage;           //The message we want to display
        int Speed;                    //Speed of the animation
        Color color = new Color(255,255,255);
        int XPos;                     //Coordinate information
        int HeightofFont;            //Font Size info
        int LengthofFont;            //Font Size info
        Font TheFont;
        Image TheImage;
        Graphics TheGraphics;

        //The init function is what gets run when the applet starts

        public void init()
        {
            //Set the basic parameters

            TextMessage = "Welcome to my web page!";
            Speed = 4;
            TheImage = createImage(1500,200);
            TheGraphics = TheImage.getGraphics();
            XPos = size().width;
            HeightofFont = 4 * size().height / 5;
            TheFont = new Font("Helvetica",1,HeightofFont);
        }

        public void paint(Graphics gfx)
        {
            paintText(TheGraphics);
            gfx.drawImage(TheImage,0,0,null);
        }
```

```
            public void paintText(Graphics gfx)
            {
                    gfx.setColor(Color.black);

                    //Make sure we are only working with our region

                    gfx.fillRect(0,0, size().width, size().height);

                    //The next line ensures only the portion of the
                    // string within the viewing rectangle will be seen

            gfx.clipRect(0,0, size().width, size().height);
                    gfx.setFont(TheFont);
                    gfx.setColor(color);
                    FontMetrics FMets = gfx.getFontMetrics();
                    LengthofFont = FMets.stringWidth(TextMessage);
                    HeightofFont = FMets.getHeight();

                    //Actually write the string to the screen

                    gfx.drawString(TextMessage,XPos,size().height -
            HeightofFont / 4);
                }

            public void start()
            {

                    //If the TickerTape isn't running, start it up...

                    if (TTapeThread == null)
                    {
                        TTapeThread = new Thread(this);
                        TTapeThread.start();
                    }
                }

            public void run()
            {
                    while(TTapeThread != null)
                    {
                        try
                        {
                            Thread.sleep(50);
                        }
                        catch (InterruptedException ie)
                        {
                        }
                        setcoordinates();
                        repaint();
                    }
                }

            public void setcoordinates()
```

```
        {

                //Update the position of where the string should start

                XPos = XPos - Speed;
                if (XPos < -LengthofFont)
                {
                        XPos = size().width;
                }
        }

        public boolean handleEvent(Event AnEvent)
        {

                //This routine will respond to mouse clicks
                //If the mouse button is pressed, the applet
                // will cycle between start and stop

                if (AnEvent.id == Event.MOUSE_DOWN)
                {
                        if (Suspended)
                        {
                                TTapeThread.resume();
                        }
                        else
                        {
                                TTapeThread.suspend();
                        }
                        Suspended = !Suspended;
                }
        return true;
        }

public void stop()
{

        //If the TickerTape is running, then make sure we stop it

        if (TTapeThread != null)
                TTapeThread.stop();
        TTapeThread = null;
        }
}
```

Here is a screen shot of the applet running from underneath the browser:

Here is the HTML page code:

```
<html>
<head>
<title>TickerTape</title>
</head>
<body>
<hr>
<applet
code=TickerTape
width=1000
height=200>

</applet>
<hr>
</body>
</html>
```

We could also modify the applet so that it reads the text message it is to print from the HTML code. There is only a little work required to do this. First, I modify the HTML code so that it has the text string as a parameter to the applet, as follows:

```
<applet
code=TickerTape
width=1000
height=200>

<param name=TEXT VALUE="Welcome to my web page!">
</applet>
```

Now, I need to modify just a bit of my program to read the parameter from my HTML page when the applet starts up. We only need to change code within the *init* routine. Here is what the new code looks like:

```
//The init function is what gets run when the applet starts

public void init()
{
     //Set the basic parameters

     //TextMessage now gets set by the parameter called text
     // in the HTML page

     TextMessage = getParameter("TEXT");
     Speed = 4;
     TheImage = createImage(1500,200);
     TheGraphics = TheImage.getGraphics();
     XPos = size().width;
     HeightofFont = 4 * size().height / 5;
     TheFont = new Font("Helvetica",1,HeightofFont);
}
```

The last sample applet that we are going to look at in this section shows how a simple *Graphical User Interface (GUI)* can be constructed to work with a Web browser. This applet will have a text box, a push button and a choice (combo) box. Here is the source code and comments for the applet AWTDemo:

```
import java.applet.*;
import java.awt.*;

public class AWTDemo extends Applet
{

    //The first two variables correspond with the physical layout of
    //  the GUI

    private GridBagLayout gbLayout;
    private GridBagConstraints gbConstraints;


    //These variables are actually the controls we are going to put
    //  into our interface

    private Choice TheChoiceBox;       //A choice (combo) box
    private TextArea TheTextArea;      //A text area
    private Button Button1;            //A button

    public void init()
    {

        //Set up the layout of the GridBag

        gbLayout = new GridBagLayout();
        setLayout(gbLayout);
        gbConstraints = new GridBagConstraints();
```

```
                        //Create a choice box and add the available options to it

                        TheChoiceBox = new Choice();
                        TheChoiceBox.add("Vanila");
                        TheChoiceBox.add("Chocolate");
                        TheChoiceBox.add("Strawberry");

                        //Create the other two controls

                        TheTextArea = new TextArea("Notes",5,10);
                        Button1 = new Button("Do It!");

                        gbConstraints.fill = GridBagConstraints.BOTH;

                        AddControl(TheChoiceBox,1,1,1,1);
                        AddControl(TheTextArea,4,5,9,15);
                        AddControl(Button1,1,7,10,8);

                }

                //This is a routine I wrote so that I wouldn't have to
                //  type this information more than once.  It gets called
                //  everytime that I want to add a control to the applet window.

                private void AddControl(Component aComponent, int row, int
        column, int width, int height)
            {
                        gbConstraints.gridx = column;
                        gbConstraints.gridy = row;

                        gbConstraints.gridwidth = width;
                        gbConstraints.gridheight = height;

                        gbLayout.setConstraints(aComponent,gbConstraints);
                        add(aComponent);
                }
        }
```

The next screen shows what the applet looks like under the browser. Notice that the choice (combo) box is open and that I can use the mouse to select one of the options. I can also push on the button with the mouse, as well as type in the text area. None of the controls are acted upon—the purpose of this applet is to show you that graphical controls exist and are fairly easy to place in an applet.

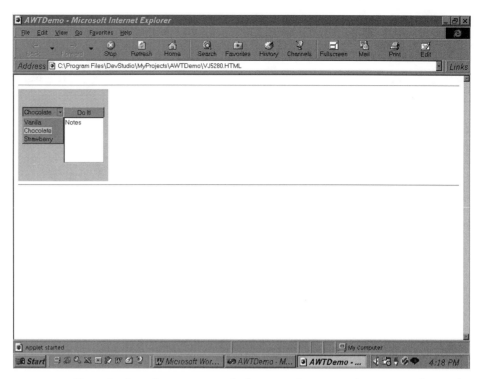

We will not look at the HTML code because there is nothing particular to this example in it.

APPLICATION:
APPLETS THAT CALCULATE

This section will examine the power of harnessing Java to create applets to solve numerical problems. In engineering and computer science, it is often necessary to compute numerical values. Instead of having to worry about carrying a calculator around or installing special software for these calculations, why not write a Java applet to do the calculations? The major advantage to this applet is that it can be run in any Java-enabled Web browser with no other special hardware or software required.

Let us create a Java applet that will solve the quadratic equation. The quadratic equation is used to solve problems in courses from precalculus through differential equations. The quadratic equation is:

$$\frac{-b \pm \sqrt{b^2 - 4 \cdot a \cdot c}}{2 \cdot a} \tag{8-2}$$

You may remember from a previous course that there are three possible solution sets for the quadratic equation:

1. There are complex (containing both imaginary and non imaginary numbers) roots, which can be determined if the discriminant (b^2-4ac) is negative.
2. There is one real root for both cases (discriminant is equal to zero).
3. There are two unique roots (discriminant is positive).

Let us develop the Java applet code necessary to solve this equation:

```java
import java.applet.*;
import java.awt.*;
import java.awt.event.*;

public class QuadApplet extends Applet implements ActionListener
{

    //Here are the variables that the applet needs

    Label GetA,GetB,GetC;    //The labels are for the prompts that
                             //  appear in front of each textfield
    TextField   TextA,TextB,TextC;  //Where the user types in values
    double      answer1,answer2,disc;   //Used for calculations
    int intA,intB,intC;                 //Converts what the user types
                                        //into integers


    public void init()
    {

        //Upon startup of the applet, create the text label and
        //  textfield for getting the number for A in the formula

        GetA = new Label("Enter A");
        add(GetA);
        TextA = new TextField(10);
        add(TextA);


        //Setup the work area for getting B

        GetB = new Label("Enter B");
        add(GetB);
        TextB = new TextField(10);
        add(TextB);


        //Finally setup the work area for getting C

        GetC = new Label("Enter C");
        add(GetC);
        TextC = new TextField(10);

        //The next line indicates that the program should do some
        //  processing when the user is finished interacting with
        //  the C textfield.  The user is done when the enter (or
        //  return) key is pressed.

        TextC.addActionListener(this);
        add(TextC);

    }
```

```
public void paint(Graphics gfx)
{

    //When this routine gets called determine the answer(s)
    //  and display them to the applet


    gfx.drawString("The answer to the quadratic equation is"
                ,1,175);
    disc = intB * intB - (4 * intA * intC);

    if (disc < 0.0)
    {
      gfx.drawString("No real solution exists",1,250);
    }
    else
    {
        answer1 = (- intB + Math.sqrt(disc)) / (2 * intA);
        answer2 = (- intB - Math.sqrt(disc)) / (2 * intA);

        if (answer1 != answer2)
        {
          gfx.drawString("2 answers: "+answer1+" and "
                        +answer2,1,250);
        }
        else
        {
          gfx.drawString("1 repeating answer: "
                        +answer1,1,250);
        }
    }

}

public void actionPerformed(ActionEvent AnEvent)
{

    //This is the routine that is called when the user
    //  is finished interacting with the C textfield


    //Convert all of the user's inputs from strings to ints

    intA = Integer.parseInt(TextA.getText());
    intB = Integer.parseInt(TextB.getText());
    intC = Integer.parseInt(TextC.getText());


    //Call the repaint function which will call paint to
    //  display the answer

    repaint();
}
}
```

Here is the HTML page code for the applet:

```
<html>
<head>
<title>QuadApplet</title>
</head>

<body>
<hr>
<applet
code=QuadApplet
width=500
height=500>

</applet>
<hr>
</body>
</html>
```

Finally, here are a couple of sample executions of the applet:

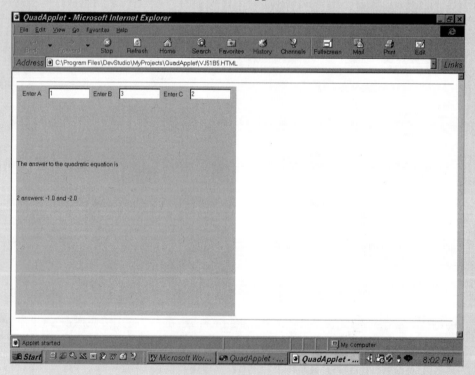

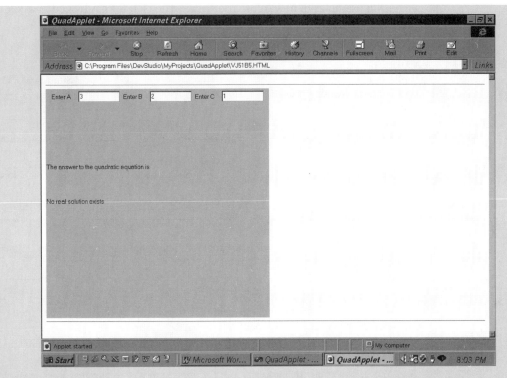

You could employ the same techniques to compute any mathematical expression. Just think of the power of constant access to such an applet. It does not matter what computer you are using, as long as you have a proper Web-browsing program. It is this kind of convenience that has pushed Java forward as a major Internet development tool.

8.6 THE FUTURE OF JAVA

The future of Java is currently skyrocketing. Many developers are flocking to Java as a solution for creating truly reusable software for multiple computer platforms. Many people believe that Java will be the ultimate language any programmer will ever need.

Not everyone believes Java will survive though. Many of the major software developers have not converted to Java because they want to see if Java will survive its infancy. In addition, Sun Microsystems, the developer of Java does not want to completely relinquish its rights to Java and make it an International Standards Organization (ISO) standard language. This mind set has provoked attacks by Microsoft, which claims that Sun is not "playing fair." Another current area of concern is that Hewlett-Packard has decided to write its own version of Java instead of using Sun's.

This splintering of the Java camp may cause Java to be like UNIX; most UNIX systems are fairly similar, but not similar enough to be completely compatible. So, every application that is supposed to run under UNIX usually requires slight modifications between systems. Is Java destined for the same situation? No one knows what the future holds in store for Java.

SUMMARY

This chapter has examined the Java programming language. This language can be used to construct both stand-alone application programs and applets, which are executed from under Web browsers. Some syntax of the basic Java language has been provided, along with examples of how to use the syntax. The chapter has looked at a couple examples of applets and has ended with a discussion on the future of Java.

KEY TERMS

Applet	GUI (Graphical User Interface)	Public
Application	If statement	Sun Microsystems
AWT (Abstract Window Toolkit)	Import	Throws
CGI	Java	UNIX
Decisions	Loops	Variables
Do-while loop	Package	Virtual Machine (VM)
Error handling	Perl	While loop
For loop	Println	

Problems

1. Write a Java application that asks for a user's name and then prints "Hello" followed by the user's name.

2. Write a Java applet that prints your name and the class title. Print out the Web page that demonstrates the applet.

3. Modify the TickerTape applet presented in the chapter so that it gets the speed setting as a parameter from the HTML page.

4. Write a Java application that is based on the mortgage calculator and prints out an amortization schedule of payments.

5. Write a Java applet that asks the user for three numbers, determines the largest of the three numbers, and prints message to the user stating which number was the largest. If all three numbers were equal, a message stating that fact should be displayed.

6. Write a Java application that uses *for loop* to print all of the numbers from 1 to 15, each number's square, and each number's cube.

7. Write a Java applet that allows a user to input either a measurement in inches or a measurement in centimeters. The applet should then convert the input measurement to the other measurement system and print the result.

8. Write a Java application that allows the user to input numbers via a loop until a negative number is input. Have your program print out the smallest number input by the user.

9. Write a Java application that allows the user to enter three nonzero integers. Check to see if the three numbers could form the sides of a right triangle. Remember that the Pythagorean theorem, $a^2 + b^2 = c^2$.

10. Write a Java application that allows the user to enter three exam scores. The three exams are each a third of the final grade. Compute the final grade from the weighed scores and determine the letter grade that the student should receive. Assume that scores greater than 90 are an A, scores greater than 80 are a B, and so on.

9

Computer Security and the Internet

SCIENCE/ENGINEERING SPOTLIGHT: N/C MACHINING AND CAM

N/C machining, or numerical control machining, is the direction of a tool to do a task through numerical data and instructions. The idea for N/C machining came about from the manufacture of helicopter blades. At the time, circa World War II, helicopter blades were made by hand, and their construction at best a trial-and-error process. N/C machining was born when it was realized that if several data points on a good blade were sampled, another decent blade could be machined with those specifications by a small group of people working together. One individual would call off x-and y-coordinate cutting information, and a couple of others would turn the machine that made the blades to the given coordinates. With the advent of computers, this process continued to get more precise and repeatable.

Computer-Aided Manufacturing (CAM) allows a computer user to generate the geometry of a part on a computer screen. The user can then simulate the machining process on the computer screen, and if everything looks correct, the user can then convert the geometrical information into N/C machining data. Once the N/C machining data has been created, the user can then send the information to the appropriate machine, insert a workpiece, and watch as the

SECTIONS

- 9.1 Password Attacks
- 9.2 Social Engineering
- 9.3 Data Interception
- 9.4 Operating System and Protocol Holes
- 9.5 Computer Viruses
- 9.6 What to Do If You Are Attacked
- Summary
- Key Terms

OBJECTIVES

After reading this chapter, you should be able to:

- Know several ways to protect your password
- List 3 ways that people intercept data
- Explain what a virus is and what to do if your computer gets one.

machine creates the part. The marriage of N/C machining and Computer-Aided Manufacturing has led to quick turnaround times in the creation of prototypes of parts and has helped reduce costly errors of misprogrammed N/C machining instructions by simulating of the cutting path on the computer screen.

Who has to worry about security on the Internet? If you are an Internet user, then you should worry. This is not to say that you need to take a paranoid stance and never use the Internet. Instead, you should be aware of the potential dangers and take the appropriate measures to keep yourself as secure as possible. We are going to examine each of the potential threats on the Internet and look into means of protecting ourselves from the threats. This chapter will examine password attacks, social engineering, data interception, operating system and protocol holes, computer viruses, and measures you can take if your security is threatened on the Internet.

9.1 PASSWORD ATTACKS

The most common way that a cracker gets into a computer system is by gaining access to someone's password. Many computer users have horrendous password habits: They make poor choices for their passwords, do not choose a password at all, or post the password on a sticky note adhered to the computer monitor, where anyone who walks by can see it. The truth of the matter is that once a cracker has access to your account, that individual effectively becomes you and has access to whatever you have access to.

You may think that you are safe on the Internet if you have a good password. After all, how would a cracker even know your username? Remember the *finger* command? *Finger* legitimately provides information about a user, including his or her username. Now the cracker has one half of the requirements to access the system in a legitimate user's name; all that remains is getting the right password.

Many sites that are new on the Internet do not realize all the holes that are in the operating system they use. For example it is possible to get a copy of the encrypted password file of some systems. Once a person has the encrypted password file, that person needs only to get a copy of the publicly available *crack* program and a dictionary. *Crack* takes each word in the dictionary, encrypts many variations of it, and sees if each variation matches the password. It is not unusual to figure out 10 to 15% of all passwords from a site by using *crack*. The time required to crack an average password file is only a couple of hours.

How do you protect yourself? Here is a checklist for password safety:

- Make sure your password is not publicly displayed, as on a sticky note attached to your computer moniter.
- Make sure you use a password as well as change that password every so often.
- Use a password that is not related to you and cannot be looked up in any dictionary.
- Use letters, numbers, and punctuation in you password. Mix the cases of the letters, if possible.
- Your password should at least be six characters long.
- Implementing one-time passwords (passwords which are only used once-the user receives a new password for each logon).
- Do not use the same password on every system to which you have access.
- If your computer comes with a boot password, use it.
- Get rid of passwords and implement of a physical hardware passkey system.

9.2 SOCIAL ENGINEERING

Social engineering is a type of attack in which a cracker attempts to gain access to a system by impersonating someone within an organization (another valid user, someone in the information-systems department, a hired consultant, etc.). A typical social-engineering attack will occur when someone calls pretending to be a system administrator who needs to log on as you to check some system parameter (access capabilities, response time, etc.). These con-jobs are carried out so gracefully that most organizations do not even know they have been hit. Even AT&T was struck by someone calling its computer department claiming to be Ken Thompson, co-inventor of Unix.

Social engineering attacks usually occur in one of two ways:

- Telephone calls
- Personal visits (Crackers have been known to rummage through trash cans looking for information that will help them get in a company; some have been bold enough to enter an organization claiming they have been hired as outside consultants).

Here is a checklist of ways by which you can protect yourself from social-engineering scams:

- Never give your password to anyone over the phone, and do not readily distribute it to people who show up in person.
- Do not leave yourself logged in while you are away from your computer.
- If you do not recognize personnel who claim to be with your organization that need to work with you and/or your computer, ask for their company I.D. card or some other form of identification.
- If a person claims that he or she has been contracted as a consultant, verify this claim with someone you know in your organization.

9.3 DATA INTERCEPTION

Data interception includes many different areas: capturing someone's username and password, gaining access to important private company data, or logging the activities carried out on a particular machine. Let us examine the common ways that crackers carry out this type of security breach.

9.3.1 Packet Sniffers

Packets are the small blocks of information that are created which contain data to be transferred between computers. Packet sniffers capture the data that is transmitted over the physical media connecting computers. This media could be wires, fiber optics, microwaves, etc. The basic idea is to target an address or group of addresses and copy every packet to a file. This file can be later examined for the information that was being transmitted. The main advantage to this security breach is that it can be carried out with almost no means of detection, and since all data must be transmitted between machines, a cracker has access to just about everything, even on computers that are considered to be "secure."

A slight twist on this theme is *IP spoofing*, in which you forge packets such that your computer appears to belong on a given network or system; hence, again, you gain access to packets that you should not have. You can protect yourself from packet sniffing in the following ways:

- There are implementations of software packages called *packet wrappers*, which essentially encrypt the original data packet at the source, put a wrapper around it with the source and destination address, and then transmit the encrypted packet to the destination computer. The destination computer then must unwrap the packet with the correct key for the data to become useable. While this method does not prevent a cracker from packet sniffing, it will not directly allow the cracker access to the original data. If a sufficient encryption package is used, this method will effectively limit what the cracker can gain from this type of security hole.

- If you can not use a packet wrapper, then at least think about encrypting your data before sending it. Some of the available packages for data encryption include DES (Data Encryption Standard), RSA (Rivest, Shamir and Adleman), and PGP (Pretty Good Privacy), which has been mentioned previously in this text.

9.3.2 Keystroke Logging

Keystroke logging occurs when, someone gathers a log of all of the keystrokes made on a particular computer. The logging may occur from a program that has been modified to send the keystrokes to their original destination as well as to a file; another alternative is to monitor the electromagnetic radiation being emitted from the computer. While this method may sound as if it comes from an episode of Star Trek, it can and has been done. Since most keyboard controllers communicate in the 15-to-25 Mhz range and the video controller is in the 40-to-50 Mhz range (according to FCC standards), anyone can purchase a radio receiver and an oscilloscope to spy on a computer. Here is a suggestion for how to protect yourself from keystroke logging:

- If your worry is the logging program, read the next section. If it is the electro-magnetic-radiation approach that has you worried, put up the appropriate shielding or purchase a TEMPEST machine. TEMPEST machines meet government and military standards to avoid having their EMR signatures read.

9.3.3 Modified Programs

There is nothing more difficult to detect than a modified program. Think of what could (and does) happen if an individual had the source to your operating system's login program. The individual could modify the code in such a way that it would echo your login name and password attempt to a file, but still pass that information on to the original part of the login program such that you can detect nothing wrong. The modifier of the program could then periodically grab a copy of that file and thus have access to most (if not all) accounts. Worse yet, there are utilities that allow you to change the file size, date and time to match the values in place when legitimate users last logged in, thereby showing no apparent change to their files. Here are some suggestions for how to protect yourself from security threat:

- You should take "snapshots" of the system periodically, recording the original file date and size. While there are utilities that can permit a cracker to modify this information, it still yields some peace of mind. If the number of files in the snapshot greatly increases or decreases, there is a possibility that some kind of a security breach has occurred.

- You may also want to get a package that computes checksums on the files on your computer. A checksum is a number that is obtained at by subjecting a file to a mathematical algorithm. Once the checksum has been computed, modifying the date and time to hide a changed program will not be enough. If the content of the program has changed, the checksum will not match against the original and will be flagged by the security program. Remember, though, for every security hole you plug, another is invented. There are software packages that generate a new checksum for the modified program and place that size in the checksum database, hiding the discovery of the modified program.

PROFESSIONAL SUCCESS: SENDING SENSITIVE INFORMATION OVER THE INTERNET

You may be interested in purchasing products over the Internet. Many sites that offer products for sale make purchasing them very easy: All you need to do is enter your credit card number and expiration date. Would you willingly give this information over the phone? If you answered no, then why are you willing to transmit this same information through numerous systems before it reaches its final destination?

Electronic commerce (e-commerce) is just starting to make some headway in providing secure ways to purchase items via the Internet. There are some "electronic banks" on line that allow you to put money in debit type of account and then purchase items with funds drawn from that account. These forms of transaction use and require highly encrypted data exchanges. In most cases, the actual transaction must be verified by some type of authentication before any funds will be transferred.

Because e-commerce is still in its infancy, you need to be careful with the business you conduct over the Internet. If you do decide to enter your credit card information, just remember that it can be intercepted and used by other people. Try to select vendors that you know are reputable and encrypt the information you transfer.

9.4 OPERATING SYSTEM AND PROTOCOL HOLES

With the complex state of today's operating systems, people are bound to make mistakes when developing the programs that make them up. Unfortunately, crackers have nothing better to do than to try to find and exploit these holes. The only safe operating system today is one that is on a computer that is never turned on! You can protect yourself from this type of security threat in the following ways:

- Many people think that when they delete a file, it is gone. In MS-DOS, there is a program called *undelete* that restores deleted files. Some vendors provide packages that write a series of the numeral one and then the numeral zero over the original file before it is deleted. This way, if an individual undeletes the file, it will be junk.

- Make sure that you have assigned the proper file permissions to your files. Operating systems such as Unix allow the owner of a file to determine who can access a file and what type of access they have to it. You should investigate this area of the operating system that you use.

- Keep up to date on patches, or remedies to operating-system errors, that are available from the operating-system vendor. Apply the patches and upgrades as soon as possible. Read any newsgroups dealing with your computer, operating system, and protocol so that you are as aware as possible of holes that have been located.

- Implement a firewall to protect your host. A firewall is a computer that you program to allow certain services and addresses in and out of your network.

Most firewalls allow you to deny ranges of addresses, protocols, ports, and services.

PRACTICE!

Do you know whether your computer system's software is up to date? Use your browser and head to the operating system manufacturer's Web site. You may be surprised by what you find. There are often patches for operating systems and Web browsers that help to make your computer system more secure when you use the Internet.

9.5 COMPUTER VIRUSES

Computer viruses are programs that have the ability to reproduce and spread across a computer system and/or network. The program may contain specific instructions that perform a destructive task if a given event occurs. Viruses typically attack executable programs and diskette boot sectors; however any piece of data that might be read into a computer's memory and executed is a possible source for transporting a virus. Even something as innocuous as Microsoft Word's Macro function has been used to transmit a virus. Viruses can attack hardware, software, and data; thus, they are bad news and can do lots of damage.

How Do You Get Viruses?

- A program is executed from an infected disk.
- A user attempts to boot from an infected disk.
- An infected program is downloaded and executed.
- An infected program is transferred over a computer network and executed.
- An infected program is specifically planted in a target computer system where it will be executed.

What are Some of the Indications of an Infection?

- Access lights turn on for devices that are not being used
- A file's size, date, or time changes unexpectedly.
- Computers unexpectedly start rebooting.
- Disk access seems excessive for simple tasks.
- Disk space is suddenly reduced.
- Files suddenly start vanishing.
- Keyboard keys do odd things or lock up.
- More marked bad spots appear on hard drives.
- New files suddenly appear.
- Programs attempt to write to write-protected disks.
- Programs take longer to load or run slower than usual.
- Strange noise or music is played over the speaker.
- The amount of available memory is decreased.
- The system can no longer properly boot up.
- There are unexplained hidden files present.
- Unusual displays or error messages appear.

Any and all of these events can be explained by programs as well as viruses. However, many of these events occurring together or repeated occurrences of several may signal viral trouble.

Programs Similar to Viruses

- Trojan horse: A program designed to look like a valid application, such as a spreadsheet or word processor. When a user runs the trojan horse, a destructive task typically occurs. For example, the user may believe he or she is saving data to a disk when, in fact, the hard drive is being reformatted instead. A trojan horse cannot reproduce itself, so it is not a virus.
- Logic bomb: A set of instructions that will activate if some given conditions are met. For example if a user runs a program to produce payroll checks and employee #953 is missing, the logic bomb erases all of the payroll data files.
- Worm: A usually benign program that spreads itself through networks. Worms usually spread through security holes in the computer's operating system and may tie up system resources until they are removed.

How to Protect Yourself

- Avoid booting your computer from floppy disks.
- Back up all original software and install only from the backup disks.
- Back up your computer system often.
- Limit the amount of software you bring from home to the office.
- Never use bootleg, hacked, or pirated software, even for evaluation purposes.
- Purchase name-brand software, and insist on buying shrink-wrapped packages only.
- Use virus scanners often, and update the scanners frequently.

PRACTICE!

Scan your computer system for viruses. You should do so often, especially if you are in an environment where a lot of people share a computer system. If you do not have a virus scanner, refer to the Science/Engineering Application in Chapter 4 to find out how to get one.

9.6 WHAT TO DO IF YOU ARE ATTACKED

If you know that you have been attacked, you may want to run through the list that follows. It is quite possible, though, that you may have been attacked but not realize it for quite a while, if ever.

What to Do If You Discover a Security Breach

- Disconnect from the Internet, and perform some housecleaning. You might have to reload your system from backups or from scratch.
- Force every user on the system to change his or her password.
- You may want to contact CERT, the Computer Emergency Response Team at Carnegie-Mellon University. The people on CERT may not be able to help you out of your trouble, but they will at least see if the attack is similar to other current attacks. CERT publishes security advisories, so your misery may help others avoid it.

SUMMARY

This chapter has examined some of the basic security issues concerning computer use and the Internet. The most commonly exploited security breach is that of taking advantage of poorly chosen passwords. The chapter has presented some suggestions on creating "good" passwords. The chapter has also examined other ways in which computer systems can be violated: social engineering, data interception, and operating system and protocol holes. Computer viruses, a continuing threat to Internet users, have been briefly studied and suggestions on ways to ward off virus attacks have been presented. The chapter has concluded with a look at what to do if a system breach is discovered.

KEY TERMS

Checksums
crack
Data interception
Infection
IP spoofing
Keystroke logging
Logic bombs

Modified programs
Operating-system holes
Packet sniffers
Packet wrappers
Password attacks
Patches
Protocol holes

Social engineering
System snapshots
TEMPEST
Trojan horse
Virus
Worm

Appendix A: The TCP/IP Protocol

In this appendix, we will take a closer look at TCP/IP and its components. We will examine the buzzwords that you will encounter when reading many Internet documents. You do not need to know any of this information to use the Internet. If you will be setting up applications on your computer, some of these issues might come up, so this section serves as a quick reference to the world of TCP/IP.

A.1 PROTOCOLS

Transport Protocols   Control the movement of data between two computers.

TCP (Transmission Control Protocol) is a connection-based service between two machines that are connected and in communication with each other at all times.

UDP (User Datagram Protocol) is a connectionless service, meaning that data can be sent and received between machines that are not currently connected or communicating with each other.

Routing Protocols   Handle the addressing of the data and determine the best way to get the data to its destination. Routing protocols are also responsible for breaking up large messages and reassembling those messages at their destination.

IP (Internet Protocol) is responsible for the actual transmission of data.

ICMP (Internet Control Message Protocol) handles status messages for IP, such as errors and changes that affect the routing of information.

RIP (Routing Information Protocol) is one of several protocols that determine the best routing method to deliver a message.

OSPF (Open Shortest Path First) is an alternative protocol for determining routing.

Network Addresses   These related protocols are used for associating IP addresses and hostnames.

ARP (Address Resolution Protocol) determines the unique (Ethernet) numeric address of machines on a network from the machine's IP address.

DNS (Domain Name Service) determines numeric addresses from machine names.

RARP (Reverse Address Resolution Protocol) determines addresses of machines, but in reverse of ARP.

User Services   These are applications that a user can run.

BOOTP (Boot Protocol) starts up a network machine by getting information from a server, such as what the machine's IP Address should be and so on.

FTP (File Transfer Protocol) transfers files between machines.

TELNET allows remote logins to other machines.

Gateway Protocols   These protocols help the network communicate routing and status information.

EGP (Exterior Gateway Protocol) transfers external network routing information.

GGP (Gateway to Gateway Protocol) transfers gateway routing information.

IGP (Internal Gateway Protocol) transfers internal network routing information.

Miscellaneous Protocols

NFS (Network File System) permits the sharing of directories and disks across a network. It allows directories on a remote computer to be accessed just as if they were local directories.

NIS (Network Information Service) allows user account information such as passwords and login names to be shared across a network, cutting down on the amount of maintenance that needs to be performed.

RPC (Remote Procedure Call) allows remote applications to communicate with each other in a simple, efficient manner.

SMTP (Simple Mail Transport Protocol) transfers e-mail between computers.

SNMP (Simple Network Management Protocol) is a service that sends status messages about the network and devices connected to it.

A.2 INTERNET ADDRESS CLASSES

When an entity gets assigned an IP Address, it will be one of three possible classes:

Class A   Starts with a number between 0 - 127

Class B   Starts with a number between 128 - 191

Class C   Starts with a number between 192 and 223

The primary difference between the address classes are the number of computers that can be put on that type of network. For example, a class-C address will have the first three triplets assigned, meaning that you can assign the last triplet for each computer that needs to be connected (roughly 255 machines). A class-B address assigns the first two triplets, leaving around 65,000 numbers that can be assigned to an organization's computers through the other two sets of triplets. Finally, a class-A address assigns only the first triplet, leaving about 16,000,000 numbers that can be assigned through the other three triplets.

Submasks Many times, software programs want to know which submask to use. Think of a submask as a question about how many machines are within an organization's class. Zero indicates all, so if you need a Class-C submask, use 255.255.255.0. For a Class-B network, use 255.255.0.0 as the submask. For a Class-A network, use 255.0.0.0 as the submask.

Appendix B: Miscellaneous Internet Programs

This appendix takes a look at some other programs that are useful when working with the Internet. These programs were not included in the main section of the text, since not all computer systems have versions of these programs available.

B.1 IP-ADDRESS RESOLVER

Sometimes it is convenient to know the IP address associated with a particular hostname. Fortunately there is an IP-address resolver that is available via e-mail. To use this service, send e-mail to *resolve@cs.widener.edu* with a blank subject line and site *hostname* as the body of the message. You will receive a reply that shows the hostname's IP address.

There are also several programs around that perform the same task. One of the more popular programs is *nslookup*.

Here is an example of the use of *nslookup*, in which I find out the IP address to the computer at Kettering called *defiant*:

```
nova{sjames}21% nslookup defiant.kettering.edu

Name: defiant.kettering.edu
Address: 192.138.137.53
```

B.2 PING

Ping is a program that is usually supplied with most TCP/IP packages. It provides you with a means of determining whether or not a given computer is accessible from your location. It does so by transmitting packets to see if it can receive them back from the other system. If it receives the packets in return, then the two systems are connected. The name "Ping" is derived from the sound that an sonar echo makes underwater. If you have ping, you can enter the ping command, followed by a machine name or IP address. If the remote machine is accessible, ping will provide you with some network statistics.

Let us trying to ping *nova* to see if it is "alive," or accessible, from *defiant*.

```
defiant:~$ ping nova.kettering.edu
PING nova.kettering.edu (192.138.137.2): 56 data bytes
64 bytes from 192.138.137.2: icmp_seq=0 ttl=255 time=1.7 ms
64 bytes from 192.138.137.2: icmp_seq=1 ttl=255 time=1.7 ms
64 bytes from 192.138.137.2: icmp_seq=2 ttl=255 time=1.6 ms
64 bytes from 192.138.137.2: icmp_seq=3 ttl=255 time=1.6 ms
64 bytes from 192.138.137.2: icmp_seq=4 ttl=255 time=1.7 ms
64 bytes from 192.138.137.2: icmp_seq=5 ttl=255 time=1.6 ms
64 bytes from 192.138.137.2: icmp_seq=6 ttl=255 time=1.7 ms
64 bytes from 192.138.137.2: icmp_seq=7 ttl=255 time=1.7 ms
64 bytes from 192.138.137.2: icmp_seq=8 ttl=255 time=1.7 ms
64 bytes from 192.138.137.2: icmp_seq=9 ttl=255 time=1.6 ms
64 bytes from 192.138.137.2: icmp_seq=10 ttl=255 time=1.6 ms
64 bytes from 192.138.137.2: icmp_seq=11 ttl=255 time=1.7 ms
64 bytes from 192.138.137.2: icmp_seq=12 ttl=255 time=2.0 ms

-- nova.kettering.edu ping statistics --
13 packets transmitted, 13 packets received, 0% packet loss
round-trip min/avg/max = 1.6/1.6/2.0 ms
```

From the output that we received, we can see that *nova* is alive and that each packet that was sent to the computer was successfully received.

B.3 TRACEROUTE

Traceroute shows you the path taken from your computer to a remote computer. This output is more informational in nature than it is useful. However, it is interesting to see just how your system communicates with one in a foreign country or some far-away location. Another use for traceroute occurs when the network connection is slow: Traceroute may indicate that an alternative route is being taken to a remote computer system because one of the normal host computers is down.

Let us look at how I get to a computer in Australia from my location in Flint, Michigan:

```
defiant:~$ traceroute monu6.cc.monash.edu.au
traceroute to monu6.cc.monash.edu.au (130.194.1.106), 30 hops max, 40 byte packets
 1 michnetrouter (192.138.137.1) 3.322 ms 3.85 ms 3.215 ms
 2 ser5.gfec.mich.net (198.110.9.9) 40.089 ms 58.899 ms 29.742 ms
 3 ser3.flint.mich.net (198.110.9.17) 72.361 ms 61.014 ms 80.031 ms
 4 198.111.116.17 (198.111.116.17) 142.633 ms 255.507 ms 205.273 ms
 5 cpe2-fddi-1.Chicago.mci.net (192.203.195.5) 176.323 ms 153.807 ms 139.514 ms
 6 borderx2-hssi2-0.WillowSprings.mci.net (204.70.104.117) 81.704 ms 132.908 ms 205.77 ms
 7 core2-fddi-1.WillowSprings.mci.net (204.70.104.65) 216.199 ms 106.716 ms
 8 * core1.SanFrancisco.mci.net (204.70.4.169) 194.972 ms 147.921 ms
 9 border2-fddi0-0.SanFrancisco.mci.net (204.70.3.162) 159.617 ms 127.378 ms 225.566 ms
10 telstra-ds3.SanFrancisco.mci.net (204.70.33.10) 154.796 ms 167.393 ms 283.497 ms
11 telstra.SanFrancisco.mci.net (204.70.204.6) 388.338 ms 413.46 ms 373.389 ms
12 Fddi0-0.pad-core1.Sydney.telstra.net (139.130.249.226) 344.235 ms 354.992 ms 387.793 ms
13 Hssi6-0.lon-core1.Melbourne.telstra.net (139.130.249.214) 334.611 ms 356.22 ms 452.099 ms
14 vic.gw.au (139.130.239.228) 341.471 ms 406.131 ms 350.333 ms
15 national.gw.au (139.130.239.54) 354.105 ms * 444.048 ms
16 vic-gw.vrn.EDU.AU (203.21.131.114) 309.91 ms 372.842 ms 2073.72 ms
17 nis-west-gw.vrn.EDU.AU (203.21.131.6) 635.058 ms 360.201 ms 333.168 ms
18 nis-east-gw.vrn.EDU.AU (203.21.131.46) 317.949 ms 553.96 ms 2468.91 ms
19 * monash-gw.vrn.EDU.AU (203.21.131.98) 304.465 ms 514.126 ms
```

```
20 clayton-gw.monash.edu.au (130.194.14.254) 545.008 ms 304.881 ms 403.691 ms
```

You can see that I go from Flint through Chicago, Willow Springs, San Francisco, Syndey, and Melbourne on my way to my destination.

Appendix C: Common Internet Items

The following is a list of some of the common documents and objects that are often mentioned when you read about the Internet. This list provides you with the site and directory where you can FTP the information from.

Item	Site	Directory
FYIs	ftp.nisc.sri.com	fyi/fyi-index.txt
Gold in Networks!	ftp.nisc.sri.com	rfc/rfc1290.txt
Gopher	boombox.micro.umn.edu	pub/gopher/
Hitchhikers Guide	ftp.nisc.sri.com	rfc/rfc1118.txt
Internet Resource Guide	nnsc.nsf.net	resource-guide/
InterNIC Resources	ds.internic.net	/rfc/fyi/std
List of FTP Sites	pilot.njin.net	pub/ftp-list/
List of Whois Servers	sipb.mit.edu	pub/whois/whois-servers.list
Network Reading List	ftp.uu.net	inet/doc/
New User's Questions	ftp.nisc.sri.com	fyi/fyi4.txt
Public Access UNIX	gvl.unisys.com	pub/nixpub/long
RFCs	ftp.nisc.sri.com	rfc/rfc-index.txt
WAIS Information	think.com	wais/
Whois Registration	nic.ddn.mil	netinfo/user-template.txt
WWW	info.cern.ch	pub/www/doc/the_www_book
Yanoff Services List	csd4.csd.uwm.edu	pub/inet.services.txt
Zen & Art of Internet	ftp.cs.widener.edu	pub/zen/

Bibliography

Cheswick, William & Steven Bellovin. *Firewalls & Internet Security*. Reading, MA: Addison-Wesley, 1994.

Dougherty, Dale & Richard Konan. *The Mosaic Handbook*. Sebastopal, CA: O'Reilly & Associates, 1994.

Frasse, Michael. *The Windows Internet Tour Guide*. Ventana Press, 1994.

Hahn, Harley & Rick Stout. *The Internet Complete Reference*. Berkeley, CA: Osborne, 1994.

Hahn, Harley & Rick Stout. *Internet Yellow Pages, 2d edition*. Berkeley, CA: Osborne, 1995.

Horton, William, Lee Taylor, Arthur Ignacio, & Nancy Hoft. *The Web Page Design Cookbook*. New York: John Wiley & Sons, 1996.

James, Scott. *Computer Virus Seminar*. 1990.

James, Scott. *Information System Security Seminar*. 1992.

James, Scott. *Unix for Engineers*. Reading, MA: Addison-Wesley, 1997.

Karpinski, Richard. *Beyond HTML*. Berkeley, CA: Osborne, 1996.

Kehoe, Brendan. *Zen and the Art of the Internet*. Englewood Cliffs, NJ: Prentice Hall, 1996.

NorthWestNet. *Internet Passport, 5th edition*. Englewood Cliffs, NJ: Prentice Hall, 1995.

O'Reilly & Associates. *Unix in a Nutshell System V Edition*. Sebastopol, CA: O'Reilly & Associates, 1992.

Que Books. *Using the Internet, 2d edition*. Indianapolis: Que, 1995.

Que Books. *Using UNIX*. Indianapolis: Que, 1990.

Index